Don't Be a Victim . . . Be a Victor!

You are in charge of your life. Don't let gossiping co-workers, meddling neighbors, or abusive people drain your energy and steal your sense of self-worth.

Learn to develop a spiritual plan of action to strengthen your self-esteem and repel negative energy. The spells in this book include practical tips for safety as well as herbal, astrological, and color correspondences to strengthen your magick.

You don't have to live a life filled with stress and fear. Reclaim your inner power and protect yourself!

To Write to the Author

If you wish to contact the author or would like more information about this book, please write to:

Silver RavenWolf
℅ Llewellyn Worldwide
P.O. Box 64383, Dept. K729-3
St. Paul, MN 55164-0383, U.S.A.

or visit Silver's website at
http://www.silverravenwolf.com

Please enclose a self-addressed stamped envelope for reply, or $1.00 to cover costs. If outside U.S.A., enclose international postal reply coupon.

Silver's Spells for

PROTECTION

Silver RavenWolf

2001
Llewellyn Publications
St. Paul, Minnesota 55164-0383

FIRST EDITION
Second Printing, 2001

Cover art by Bill Cannon
Cover design by Anne Marie Garrison
Editing and book design by Rebecca Zins
Illustrations by Shelly Bartek (except pages 62 and 65 by Llewellyn Art Department)

Library of Congress Cataloging-in-Publication Data
RavenWolf, Silver, 1956–
    [Spells for protection]
    Silver's spells for protection / Silver RavenWolf. —1st ed.
        p.   cm.
    Includes bibliographical references and index.
    ISBN 1-56718-729-3
    1. Magic.   2. Self-preservation—Miscellanea.   I. Title.
BF1621.R38   2000
133.4'4—dc21   99-058550
                                           CIP

Llewellyn Worldwide does not participate in, endorse, or have any authority or responsibility concerning private business transactions between our authors and the public.

  All mail addressed to the author is forwarded but the publisher cannot, unless specifically instructed by the author, give out an address or phone number.

Disclaimer: These spells are not to be used in lieu of professional advice.

Llewellyn Publications
A Division of Llewellyn Worldwide, Ltd.
P.O. Box 64383, Dept. K729-3
St. Paul, MN 55164-0383, U.S.A.

 Printed in the United States of America on recycled paper

Other Books by Silver RavenWolf

In the *Silver's Spells* Series

This book is dedicated to:

members of our law enforcement and
emergency service personnel,
Pagan and otherwise

Contents

About Silver . . .

"The best way for a magickal person to be accepted is to let people get to know you," explains Silver. "Once they understand your personal values and principles, their attitudes about your alternative religion interests tend to be more positive. Let them know you for the work that you do." Silver RavenWolf is a true Virgo who adores making lists and arranging things in order. The mother of four children, she will celebrate her twentieth wedding anniversary in 2000.

Silver extensively tours the United States, giving seminars and lectures about magickal religions and practices. She has been interviewed by the *New York Times* and *U.S. News & World Report.* It is estimated that Silver has personally met over 25,000 magickal individuals in the last five years.

Silver is the Clan Head of the Black Forest Family that includes fifteen covens in eleven states. Visit her website at:

http://www.silverravenwolf.com

1

✩Operating
Instructions

As you read each line and spell

Learn one lesson very well

It's not the words or chants you do

It's not the tools that see you through

They simply help you work your plan

While all the power is in your hand

And words and deeds may play a part

But Magick lives within the heart!

—David Norris ©1998

We live, for good or ill, in an aggressive society. We may bounce along without a care in the world for several months (or perhaps even years) without a major crisis. But we cannot escape forever. Eventually the aggressive nature of human-kind steps forward in an area of our lives and challenges us. For those of relatively peaceable intent, this is such a shock that it may take precious time to marshal thoughts and abilities to meet this challenge. Some of these challenges are meant to be—they will help us grow and cast off worn behaviors that no longer meet our needs. They urge us to move from a bad situation into one that will be more spiritual, or help us meet the goals or missions of this lifetime. Other challenges we are truly meant to avoid, which is where preventative protection magick comes into play. These challenges are not for us. The lessons of prevention teach us how to work around such conflicts.

Living a Protected Life

The first step to living a protected existence lies in your desire to exercise your right to be in control of your own life. That's right. You are no longer a victim, you are a victor! Protection magick deals with your state of mind and your common sense, meaning that you don't go out drinking at 3:00 A.M., then walk down the street in the worst part of town half looped and slinging an amulet for protection around your head like a warrior's slingshot. If you do that, you are just asking for trouble—and the universe may kindly oblige you.

What This Book Is For

This book is designed to teach you how to prevent bad things from occurring and how to protect yourself should you walk into something that you shouldn't have. I'm not saying that unfortunate events are never going to happen to you; that would be silly. What I'm trying to impress on you is that there are ways to protect yourself both physically and spiritually. You can learn to avoid random acts of chaos and, in the event you are sucked into a fray, be better prepared to handle some of the challenges that may stand steadfastly in your way. If you practice the techniques in this book, then you have a better chance of living a more harmonious life. The techniques herein, however, should not preclude obtaining professional assistance, whether we are talking about the need to notify the police, a counselor, or medical professionals.

Balance

Although the discussion of balance is important in any class on magick, it is doubly important here. All workings of magick and ritual create energies to push or pull life into balance. The more your life is out of balance, the harder things will be pushed or pulled to get you back to a harmonious state. What does this mean in plain English? Well, sometimes things will appear to get worse before they get better.

When situations are really bad, some people hesitate to work protection magick because they think they've gotten themselves in so deep, *nothing* will get them out. Other people fear change, thinking the choice of dealing with the difficulty is far better than a new type of life. When you practice magick to push away the negativity of others, or the negativity of your environment, or to bring a positive lifestyle toward you, you are massaging the energies of the universe in an effort to create balance, and change—sometimes radical—is inevitable.

The Length of a Magickal Application

The actual performance of a magickal application may take as little as thirty seconds or as long as an hour. For example, although I can walk around my house with pickling salt to create a protective barrier against negativity reaching my family in less than five minutes, it will take me longer to work magick for a friend who is going through a nasty divorce. The length of the working does not necessarily ensure the success of the working.

In magick, if a particular spell doesn't work for you the first time around, don't have heart failure. Try again. The complication of the procedure carries less importance than the finesse of the procedure. Your skill makes the application fall into the beginner or advanced category.

Manifesting and Banishing Energies

I mentioned earlier that magick represents your efforts of pushing universal energies or pulling universal energies. You push negative energies away from you. You pull positive energies toward you. Therefore, magickal individuals work two kinds of positive magick: manifesting or banishing. To manifest something is to make that something happen. To banish something is to make that something go away.

Correspondences

Most magickal applications contain correspondences. Correspondences are items or energies that relate to the focus of the issue. In this book, our focus is on protection. Throughout the book I've provided various correspondences for each spell. I've also given you a few lists in the appendices to aid you in substitutions or in the creation of your own spells.

Correspondences here include planetary hours, deities, herbs, oils, basic astrology, angels, totem animals, magickal alphabets, phases of the moon, colors, and elements. Remember, you don't have to use all the correspondences I mention in any spell. If you're not into angels, then don't use those listed. If you don't particularly like to use plant energies, then feel free to think of a different ingredient. Substitutions are acceptable. I simply tried to give you a wide range of choices that have worked for me.

Timing

Many Witches use the phases of the moon in the timing of their magickal applications. Although there are eight separate phases of the moon, we will primarily work with five specific phases:

New Moon—Beginnings

Full Moon—Power

Dark of the Moon—Banishing

Waxing—Building

Waning—Reworking or rebuilding

How long will it take your spell to manifest? How long do you have to wait before something happens? You'll have to wait as long as it takes. Don't have such a long face! Here are a few guidelines on timing:

- Magick follows the path of least resistance, so unless you have a reason for guiding the magick along a particular line of thought, just let the magick go. The more blocks you place in the way of manifestation, the longer it will take to make things happen; however, this does not mean that you shouldn't be specific in your petition.

- Small goals normally (but not always) manifest faster than large goals. For example, putting the salt around my property has an immediate effect, but working on a court case may take weeks, or even months. Normally, small goals require twenty-four hours to thirty days to manifest (or one full moon cycle). If your small goal does not happen in thirty days, work again. Witches call this technique moon to moon, as the cycle from a full moon to a full moon (or a new moon to a new moon) is approximately twenty-eight days.

- Larger goals require the building of your magickal techniques. It may be necessary to work various types of magick each week to accomplish your overall goal.

- Magick for situations and events that involve many people will normally take longer to manifest than an event having only one or two players. Each individual involved in the situation will have an agenda (hidden or otherwise) that may be working against your ultimate success. You actually need to sit down and determine who the major players are in any drama, and one unseen player. There is always someone, somewhere, who is not the most vocal and who is assisting in creating the negativity.

- Situations that are double or triple-tiered need to be separated, worked on independently, and then a working for the overall outcome should be performed. For example, your teen was suspended from school based on (1) a lie from another student, and (2) those in authority not listening to the truth. There are two agendas here, not one, even though the event culminated in one final action, and you may be able to resolve one aspect of the situation faster than another. In our example, it may take thirty days to expose the student, but sixty or ninety days until you can work through the "system" and win. Or, conversely, you may have to win first with the authorities before Karma crashes down on the head of the fibbing kid, who is now forced to step forward and tell the truth.

• The old teachers said, "Do a spell, then forget it." These teachers meant do the spell, but don't worry about it. Feeding negative thoughts into your spellwork will defeat your purpose. If you worry about the manifestation of the spell, then you create blocks in the path of that manifestation.

Keep in mind that your sincerity and needs carry important weight when casting protection spells. If today is Wednesday, and the spell calls for completion on a Saturday, but you really need to do the spell today, then go ahead and do the spell today. If the spell calls for a supply that you don't have, that's okay. Substitute something else.

Learning to Devise a Spiritual Plan

Throwing magick at a problem or goal isn't the ultimate solution to all of our difficulties. Magickal people think carefully before choosing a magickal technique or spell. You need to consider an entire plan of action, of which magick becomes a part. Yes, a spell can take only a few minutes to do, a prayer a moment or two to utter, but without a complete spiritual plan you may be throwing snowflakes at a campfire. A complete spiritual plan includes:

- Logically thinking about the goal or situation.

- Considering how your actions, both magickal and normal, will affect the outcome of the goal, situation, or other people.

- Building positive reinforcement around you.

- Reprogramming your mind to accept success through thought, word, and action.

- Involving Spirit as much as possible in what you do.

- Listing the magickal and mundane actions needed to manifest your goal.

- Listing all the players in the drama, and how you think they relate (or don't) to the situation at hand. This is especially important when we are meeting a challenge that requires protection magick.

I know all this seems a little complicated for something like a simple spell, but if we learn to plan wisely, we have a better chance of success. Many of the spells in this book can be linked together to help you design a spiritual plan.

Self-Blessing Ritual

I've found the use of a self-blessing ritual before employing magick to be incredibly helpful in focusing your mind on the task at hand. You can write your own self-blessing ritual, or you can use the one below.

Instructions: Take three deep breaths. Imagine a silver light flowing through your body. This is the energy of our Moon Goddess. Take three deep breaths. Imagine a gold light flowing through your body. This is the energy of the Sun God. Take three deep breaths. Imagine a white light flowing through your body. This is the combined energy of the Universal Life Force or Universal Love. Say the following:

Blessed be my feet that walk the path of mystery.
Blessed be my knees that kneel at the sacred altar.
Blessed be my heart formed in beauty and love.
Blessed be my mouth that speaks the sacred names.

Open your arms wide to reach out for protection and love. Close your arms slowly across your heart to signal that you have accepted these gifts. Then say:

So mote it be.

* * *
✶ 15 ☽✶

Be Honest with Yourself

Much of protection magick involves our relationships with other people, known and unknown to us. Always be completely honest with yourself. View the situation as fairly as possible. If you have any doubt, ask a trusted friend. "Am I wrong in feeling . . . ?" is an okay question to ask. Be sure that you are not directly responsible for any negative acts against others or yourself. If you try to work magick to get yourself out of the spot you are responsible for, the magick may simply not work, or it may work in a manner you didn't expect. Remember, magick balances all things, and some situations occur because we needed to rise to the challenge to become a better, stronger person.

Feeding Negativity—Is It Worth It?

Learn to laugh at what I call "reindeer games"—you know, those silly situations where an individual purposefully tries to make your life difficult because they have low self-esteem, and therefore, you are just as good a target as any, or perhaps your life is going pretty good, so therefore you are wearing a big target on your you-know-what. Like the famous guy says, "Don't sweat the small stuff." Although this negativity can occur in almost any age group or environment, I've noticed that you are more likely a target if:

- You deal with large numbers of people (a big office environment, school, politics, religious activities).

- You are an inherently social person.

- You are well-liked and generous.

- You are attractive (inside and out).

Conversely, this can happen if:

- You have a big mouth.

- You stick your nose in where it doesn't belong.

- You are opinionated.

- You have a victim mentality.

Feeding the negativity sent to you by making a big deal out of it, worrying about it, or blowing it out of proportion can only make matters worse. I say to my kids, "If a million people in China aren't going to care about this issue, why do you?" Sometimes we can stop negative circumstances simply by thinking rationally, adjusting our behavior, and going on with our lives. If we get too caught up in the drama, then we may be creating more negativity than the situation blossomed in the first place.

Why Magick Doesn't Always Work

Sometimes Spirit knows better than we do what will be right for us. I've always taught my students and my children that if your magick doesn't work, if your spiritual plan fails, do not lose confidence in yourself. Spirit knows what you need and what you don't, and sometimes, when you are least expecting it, Spirit will step in and bring your work to a grinding halt. Sometimes Spirit does this to protect us, and other times Spirit knows that we have bigger missions, larger goals, and more important activities that we should be doing.

I've taught my children to ask Spirit during a magickal working "to make the best thing happen for me." This way, you allow Spirit to help guide you in your work and play.

Don't Look for Black Magick

I've also learned something else that's very important. If strange things start happening around you, don't look for black magick, look for the activity of Spirit. The universe is definitely trying to tell you something. You may be on the wrong path, you may have made an unfortunate turn some-where, perhaps your friends aren't who you thought they were and their activities bring negativity into your life, or you may be spending time on something that would be wasteful to your purpose. Sometimes, Spirit has to hit us over the head with a giant broomstick to get us to pay attention. Once we wake up, we can correct our activities and focus on what would be best for us, rather than tying ourselves to a self-created illusion.

The Dark Side—Magickal People Don't Go There

Intelligent magickal people don't work magick to harm others because they know that no real power lies in evil. I've seen people that look to the dark side, thinking that Witches who do good are weak, and therefore good poses no threat against evil. Oh, please—spare me! Think again. Although magickal individuals understand that the world contains order and chaos, and that both energies work together in the universe to create our world, chaos does not mean evil, and real Witches never, ever get involved with evil.

Am I saying that you can't fight back if someone has hurt you? Not at all. But I am saying that there will be times in your life where you are going to get really, really mad at some sort of injustice. Practicing evil does not negate someone else's evil. Instead, we learn to banish that evil and work with Karma, rather than adding negative Karma to our own pot.

With these general operating instructions under your magickal belt, it is time to flex those fingers and dig into practical protection!

2
Personal Prevention Magick

When you practice magick, you are orchestrating an individual tune that vibrates throughout the universe. Protection magick establishes energy barriers between yourself and the negativity (such as negative people, negative energies, etc.) and either pushes or pulls manifestations toward you or away from you in the manner that you specify.

Preventative protection magick offers us the following opportunities:

- Strengthens our self-esteem.

- Catches and deflects situations that we may have consciously overlooked.

- Fills us with a sense of responsibility for our own actions, and reminds us that as we sow, so shall we reap.

- Leads us away from the victim mentality.

- Allows us to better control our environment.

- Increases our productivity through focus of thoughts, feelings, and desires by removing some of our daily fears (real or imagined).

- Puts us in touch with our personal choice of divinity.

Are You Sending the Wrong Message?

Whether we're talking about love, money, or success, there is a certain element of our society that looks for victims. These horrid people consider themselves predators, and you (my little pretty) have been sized-up on numerous occasions to determine if you fit within the parameters of the victim profile. Let's face it, even serial killers buy groceries. The way you walk, talk, and interact with others gives the predator enough information to determine if you are a delicate morsel waiting to be seized or a tough old bird too difficult to bother plucking.

The spells in this chapter all fall under the heading of preventative magickal practices—those workings that you do before a challenge or opposition occurs. I've also divided these workings into topics. However, just because I've applied a magickal technique to a "self" topic doesn't mean you can't use that technique for a "social" topic. Feel free to mix and match the spells, rituals, or techniques to the focus you desire.

Clarity Spell

Here's a spell to help you think first and speak with clarity later. Although most often used for potions of passion and love, sugar (especially brown sugar) works extremely well in protection spells. Although most magickal people scatter salt around their homes as a protective device, one could use brown sugar; however, with summer ants and other little buggies that like sugar, this may not be a wise idea (at least inside your house or apartment). The color brown has two primary associations, although there are others—one vibrational use is for sympathy between two parties or two issues. Another use is for protection, and some magickal individuals prefer using brown although a spell may call for the color black.

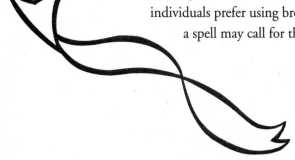

Supplies: Brown sugar; bowl; brown votive candle; your
name on a piece of paper; a brown ribbon, 13 inches
long; a lock of your hair tied or glued into the ribbon.

Instructions: Put the candle in the bowl. Surround with
brown sugar (to bring sweet things to you). On the piece
of paper, write your name and the words "Wisdom and
Power." Hold your hands over the unlit candle, and say:

> Holy Mother, bring to me words of power,
> so that whenever I utter any word the thoughts
> behind it contain kindness and clarity.
> Bless me with inner wisdom.

Light the candle. Take a deep breath and see yourself
being happy and wise. Be sure to capture that feeling-
good emotion. Envision yourself speaking with clarity
and grace. Tie seven knots in the ribbon, saying:

> With knot of one, this spell's begun.
> With knot of two, my wish comes true.
> With knot of three, wisdom enter me.
> With knot of four, I fear no more.

With knot of five, this spell's alive.
With knot of six, my words are quick.
With knot of seven, power's given!
With harm to none. So mote it be!

Stand at the outskirts of the room and begin to walk in a
clockwise direction in circles (you will be walking in a
spiral) until you reach the center of the room. Hold the
ribbon up over your head and proclaim (aloud) your
wisdom and your power! Ask for blessings from the
Holy Mother. (**Note:** You can use this spiral
walk to enhance any spell.)

Allow the candle to burn out. (Be sure you are doing
this in a safe place.) Bury the brown sugar and the
remaining candle (if any) in your back yard. Keep the
ribbon with you. Anytime you feel nervous, hold it
and repeat in your mind, "My words carry great
wisdom and power."

Next time someone attacks you verbally, or you want to
attack them, ask yourself this Jungian question before
you speak, "Is God/dess inside? Or is God/dess outside?"
and then speak—from the heart.

To enhance this spell:

• Perform on a Sunday for success.

• Perform in the hour of the sun (see planetary hour appendix).

• Perform on Beltaine (May Day).

• Add gold or silver glitter to the brown sugar to assist in drawing shining energies toward yourself.

• Perform on the new moon or the full moon.

• Perform on Wednesday for communication.

• Ask the assistance of the sylphs (energies of the east quarter).

• Perform on Tuesday if someone is attacking you (Mars energy).

• Use during a Mars retrograde (which happens every two years) to contemplate how you would like to improve yourself. Determine a plan of action, and then carry out that plan after Mars turns direct.

Practical Tip

With every nice thing we say, we increase the positive energy around us and therefore enhance our protection, health, and success in any venture. With every mean thing we say, we increase the negative energy around us. Scary thought, huh? It's very important to feel comfortable with who and what we are, because our words and actions communicate to the world around us how we feel about ourselves.

Avert Disaster Planned by Others

Coffee contains caffeine, which can help to avert negativity through your direct action.

Supplies: ½ cup coffee; 1 stick pure, unsalted butter; the names of those who stand against you, written on a small slip of paper; 1 coffee filter; 1 small bowl.

Instructions: Place the coffee filter in the small bowl. Draw any magickal signs or runes on the filter that you

feel would be appropriate, or write the name of your
chosen god or goddess. The double-headed god Janus
works well for this particular magickal working.

Heat the butter. Remove sediments. You only want the
clear liquid, called ghee. Strain this liquid.

Place the names of the individuals against you on top of
the filter, followed by the coffee grounds. Pour warm
ghee over the mixture. Call on Janus for assistance in
removing these individuals from your life. When the
spell is completed, dispose of the mixture off your
property. As the mixture rots, those individuals will
be removed from your life.

Black Madonna Protection Incense

When burned, incense is your gift to Spirit. The fragrant
smoke also helps to put you in a calm, relaxed state of mind.
There are a variety of recipes throughout this book that you
may like to use in conjunction with a spell, or to burn "just
because."

Probably the most well-known of the Egyptian goddesses,
Isis represents ceremonies, immortality, time, astrology,

earth, nature, moon, and night. She holds a number of titles (Queen of the Earth, Mother of the Seasons, and Protectress of the Dead). She was worshiped throughout Egypt, the Roman Empire, Chaldea, Greece, Germany, Gaul, and many other areas—a very encompassing feminine energy. With Rome's occupation of outlying territories came the expansion of Isis worship. With the advent of Christianity, many of the chapels in Europe dedicated to Isis changed the representations of this goddess holding her son, Horus, to the Virgin Mary carrying Jesus. Because Isis was dark-skinned, these representations became known as the Black Virgins or Black Madonnas. These Black Madonnas have been discovered on most continents: Europe (France, Germany, Italy, Poland, Spain, and Switzerland), the Americas (Mexico, Central America, and South America), Africa, Asia, and the Pacific.[1]

---

1. Martha Ann Imel and Dorothy Myers, *Goddesses in World Mythology, A Biographical Dictionary* (New York: Oxford University Press, 1993).
2. Morgana is the proprietor of Morgana's Chamber, a Witchcraft shop at 242 West 10th St., NY, NY 10014; (212) 243-3415; website: members.aol.com/MorganasCh. Her specialties are handmade incense from her personal recipes, carved magical candles, and herbal magick. She is a member of the Black Forest Family.

The following incense protection formula was designed by Morgana.[2]

Supplies: ½ cup coarsely ground cedar chips; 1 tablespoon coarsely ground myrrh resin; ½ tablespoon finely ground dragon's blood resin; 11 drops lily oil (lotus oil may be substituted); 5 drops rose oil; ½ teaspoon crushed vervain; a few crushed rose petals.

Instructions: Start with cedar shavings, adding ingredients in the order given above. Mix well after each addition. Concentrate on the protective energy of Isis while mixing. Store in a jar or plastic bag. Add to charcoal to burn. As you begin to burn the incense, hold your hands over the smoke, and say:

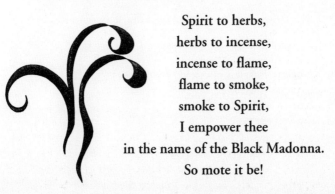

Spirit to herbs,
herbs to incense,
incense to flame,
flame to smoke,
smoke to Spirit,
I empower thee
in the name of the Black Madonna.
So mote it be!

Protecting My Body (Shielding)

One of the most important techniques any magickal individual should learn incorporates a process called shielding that repels negative energy. There are several ways to do this, from learning the simple white-light technique to the more complicated procedures. It is important that you choose the technique that is right for you and stick with it.

Shielding is primarily the act of practiced visualization. Here are some ideas to help you (practice five minutes each day):

- Envision yourself encircled in pure white light.

- Envision yourself encircled by angelic wings.

- Envision yourself encircled by a dense hedge.

- Envision yourself encircled by a force field.

- Envision yourself encircled by mirrors that face outward, away from you.

Four Directions Protection Spell

For this spell we use the Lunate Cross, which defends the
center (you) with crescent moons directed outward. This
particular sign was popular with European shamans.[3] In
alchemy, this sign stands for vinegar. (**Note:** Although we are
using this symbol in a protective ritual here, you can inscribe
the design on a black candle, dress in vinegar, and place over
your picture to stave off future attacks from someone who
has turned negative energy toward you.)

Goddess energy for this spell is Luna, Roman goddess of
the moon, night, and time, meaning if you want to put a
more complicated twist into your magickal working by desig-
nating a specific amount of time, Luna will oblige you.
Luna's name means "the moon that rules the months" and
she is associated with the seasons as well as the first day of the
waning moon. Her holiday is March 31.

Supplies: The four aces in any poker deck; a black marker.

---

3. Barbara Walker, *The Woman's Dictionary of Symbols and Sacred
Objects* (San Francisco: Harper San Francisco, 1988), p. 55.

Lunate Cross

Instructions: Draw the Lunate Cross with the black marker over the face of each card. Cast a magick circle. Place the aces in the following manner: club in the north (money, wealth, work, luck); diamond in the east (courage, energy, daring); spade in the south (destiny, logical thinking); heart in the west (love, family, growth). You can illuminate the four quarters with votive candles if you desire (green: north; yellow: east; red: south; blue: west).

Envision yourself surrounded by white light. Call forth
the assistance of Luna. Feel the power of her spirit
encompass you. Walk to the north, hold the ace of clubs,
and say:

**By the power of the north
protective energy, now flow forth.**

Keep the card in your hand and walk to the east. Hold
the ace of diamonds, and say:

**By the power of the east
bring wisdom within my reach.**

Keep the cards in your hand and walk to the south.
Hold the ace of spades, and say:

**By the power of the South
I do not fear, nor do I doubt.**

Keep the cards in your hand and walk to the west. Hold
the ace of hearts, and say:

By the power of the west
ebb and flow, and coalesce.

Walk to the center. Hold the four aces over your head, and say:

Protection around me, above me, below me,
from all directions, love and hold me.
By the power of the One[4]
Lord and Lady it is done!
So mote it be!

Glue the four aces together and keep in pocket or purse for continued protection. Thank the goddess Luna.

----

4. "One" as in the combined power of the Lord and Lady, or Spirit.

Practical Tip

So everybody doesn't like you? So what? As long as you are not doing things to hurt people, their opinion of you should not matter. Likewise, you need to monitor what you say about others. Sometimes we don't realize that the words or feelings we communicate can harm people, simply because we didn't think about what was coming out of our mouths (or, in the case of the Internet, off our fingers). It's one thing to have an opinion, it is another to humiliate people by calling them names or attempting to denigrate them to make yourself feel better.

Dragon's Eye Triangle

For a negative circumstance to occur (whether we are talking about an immoral or criminal action), three elements must be present: desire, ability, and opportunity. The easiest way to stop a negative action before it happens is to eliminate the opportunity. The simplest way to eradicate the opportunity is to use the best defensive weapon you have: your mind. Most actions against us, whether it is your mother-in-law ripping on you or the guy standing too close to you at the ATM, happen when we aren't paying attention. Things are going well and we become complacent, and that's when the predator strikes!

Every morning, why not concentrate on your own triangle of protection? In magick, most three-way motifs, including the triangle, represent the female principle. The Goddess was the original trinity, followed later by patriarchal forms. From Australian aborigines to the original Goddess of India (Trimurti), the triangle was viewed as the focus of the spiritual universe, and was often associated with creative intellect.

The dragon's eye triangle is a triple triangle used to invoke the Goddess in her nine-form (the muses or the nine Morrigans). For protection, we employ the Morrigan, or Dark

Mother of the Celtic peoples (who was originally, I might add, an earth goddess, not a battle one). The dragon's eye triangle also has Germanic associations (called the eye of fire), and was the alchemical sign for the four elements combined.[5]

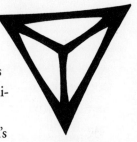

Dragon's Eye Triangle

Each morning, simply draw the dragon's eye triangle over your reflection in the glass as you get ready for work or recreation. Ask for the protection of the Divine Goddess as well as for the gift of discernment so that you won't walk blindly into any negative situations. Incorporate the four elements if you desire.

Other ways to use the dragon's eye triangle:

- On your mail.

- Sew the design onto your clothes.

- Put in decoration form on your front door.

- Carve into candles for other protection spells.

---

5. Carl G. Liungman, *Dictionary of Symbols* (New York: W. W. Norton and Company, 1991), p. 294.

Dragonbane Protection Oil[6]

Protection oils are used to anoint candles, talismans, windows, doors, favorite objects, and so on to enhance the purity of spiritual vibrations. This one is best made on the dark moon.

Supplies: 1 dram bottle; sweet almond oil; 3 drops amber oil; 1 drop jasmine oil; 7 drops dark musk (plain musk can be substituted); 5 drops rue oil; 3 small pieces dragon's blood resin; 1 pinch coarse sea salt.

Instructions: Fill dram bottle halfway with sweet almond oil. Add each oil, shaking gently to mix well. Add dragon's blood resin and sea salt. Shake to mix. Charge. When anointing an oil, you can use the following spoken charm:

> **Spirit to oil, oil to candle, candle to flame,
> flame to smoke, smoke to Spirit.**

----

6. Created by Morgana of Morgana's Chamber.

Your Internal Warning System

According to the National Law Enforcement Memorial Fund, more police officers are killed:

- Between the hours of 8 P.M. and 10 P.M.

- On Friday evenings.

- In the months of January and December.

Obviously, if more police officers are killed during these times, then it would behoove us as magickal citizens to pay attention.

Although this may sound like oversimplification, I learned a long time ago that an easy way to ensure removing chaotic events from my life was to simply ask Spirit (or whatever you believe in as the All who runs the universe) to guide me away from harmful people and events if at all possible. This works very well, IF you listen to your gut instincts, which is how Spirit usually talks to us in these matters (though some of us may be lucky enough to get louder warnings).

Your body does contain an Internal Warning System that sends a message to your beta awareness center (the state of mind you are usually in when walking, talking, or doing an activity). This warning system actually begins in the theta state of mind (although some scientists believe it comes from an even deeper recess), bips through the alpha awareness, and then is spewed into beta, often through emotional impulses or feelings. If we harness these feelings of unrest or nervousness without trying to determine the cause, then we aren't paying attention to our private Internal Warning System (IWS). Police officers and military personnel learn to listen to the human IWS. They have to. If they don't, they die. Your IWS is just as potent. If you pay attention you will soon learn who is lying to you, and even why. It just takes your willingness to be observant to the messages you receive from your own body.

Yes, Virginia, there is a reason why your skin is crawling while the guy with crazy eyes is talking to you. And all this stuff about women's intuition? Fellas have it, too.

The Witches' Girdle

Not to be mistaken with the cords of a traditional Witch, the Witches' girdle is a folk magick practice thought to be a means to seal off one's aura and prevent mental and physical attacks.[7] When I visited Missouri several years ago, many of the local Witches talked about the "Witches' girdle," and I finally found the origins of this practice in local folk magick, thanks to a dedicated researcher in the 1930s who took the time to write down a large compendium of information about the Ozark Mountain people.

Supplies: A red cord the length of your body (a favorite belt may be substituted).

Instructions: When the moon is full, raise the cord to the heavens and entreat the Lord and Lady to empower the cord with protective energy. Say:

**Spirit to cord, cord to Witch, Witch to Spirit,
I empower thee in the names of the Lord and Lady.
Bring to me joy, peace, and reverence.**

----

7. Vance Randolph, *Ozark Magic and Folklore* (New York: Columbia University Press, 1974).

Each morning, before you put on the cord, hold the cord (or belt) to the rising sun, asking for divine presence in your life and blessings upon yourself and the day. Tie the cord around your middle, using a square knot to secure. The knot should ride in the center of your abdomen.

Practical Tip

Never give your credit card, phone card, social security, or bank account number to anyone over the phone. It is illegal for telemarketers or mail marketers to ask for this information. Beware of 900 numbers. Check out all charities before donating, and ask for a financial report. Investigate before you invest. Don't ever give your Internet password to anyone, and change it frequently to numbers or letters that do not in any way relate to your life (birth date, family member names, etc.). Use an answering machine to screen your telephone calls.

Sea Salt Protection Bath [8]

Spiritual baths are excellent to rid physical and astral bodies of negativity, and to encompass your mind with relaxing energy. We'll talk a little more about spiritual baths in the following chapter.

Supplies: ½ cup Epsom salts; ⅛ cup coarse sea salt (finely ground sea salt can be substituted); 5 drops sandalwood oil; ⅛ teaspoon finely ground (to a powder) dragon's blood resin; ½ teaspoon crushed lavender; 7 drops red food coloring.

Instructions: Mix Epsom salts and sea salt well. Add ingredients, one at a time, mixing well after each addition. Add food coloring. Store in a jar, and tie with a red ribbon. Charge. Best made on a new moon. To use, add two tablespoons to running water.

----

8. Designed by Morgana of Morgana's Chamber.

Spells for Protecting Your Stuff

You may not own a diamond tennis bracelet or a Mickey Mantle baseball card but, all the same, your stuff is important to you. Con artists are smart, aggressive, and persuasive. If a fraud "looked like" a fraud, then (obviously) no one would fall for a fraud. Unfortunately, people lose millions of dollars to swindles every year. From the telephone to the doorbell, a con artist has numerous ways to enter your life and dance off with your hard-earned cash dressed like a bank examiner, a bum, a service repairperson, or in any number of costumes and disguises. The old adage "If it sounds too good to be true, it is too good to be true" should be your magickal motto.

Penelope's Protection Web

Using Penelope's web to stop fraud doesn't mean that you are to cease being observant when it comes to protecting yourself or your property; however, it is an excellent charm that works in tandem with your good sense, especially if you transform the design onto a small mirror that can be placed under your telephone, in your safety deposit box, or under your front or

Penelope's Web

back doormat. Crossing-line designs are often used in protection as the lines confuse negative energies, forcing them to
lose focus and eventually burst apart or slowly fade away.

Penelope's web design is a pattern of interlocking pentacles
composed of only two lines. The defensive ring of twenty
outward points (much like the philosophy behind a Pennsylvania Dutch hex sign) protects the wearer or one's property.

Penelope's name means "Veiled One." She is a Fate goddess, responsible for determining one's destiny. Mother and consort of Pan, Penelope acts as a personal guardian angel when needed. She is said to have refrained from cutting the thread of Odysseus' life so that he couldn't die.

By surrounding this design with a crushed, protective herb, you are further insuring protection of any one or anything, especially if you find yourself in a desperate situation. Place a picture of the individual who needs protection on the center of your altar. Cover with Penelope's web. Surround with one or a combination of the following: myrrh, rue, patchouli, or rosemary (herbs magickally associated with protection). If you don't have any of these items, regular table salt will do. Utter your own words of power, entreating Penelope to assist you. You can also enlarge the drawing in this book on a copy machine and write the letters of your first name in between the spokes of the wheel for added protection for yourself, or write down the name of the item you wish to protect evenly spaced among the spokes of the design. Laminate and carry with you as a protective device, especially if you think you are walking into a shady business deal.

To enhance this spell:

• Perform on a Saturday.

• Perform on a full moon.

• Place your personal sigil on the back of the drawing.

• Sew into an expensive piece of clothing (like your winter coat that cost you $500).

Too Hot to Touch Spell

Okay, you've been a very smart person and you don't swing your purse over your head when you walk down the street. You don't put your wallet on the counter in the dry-cleaning store while you search your pockets for your ticket. You remember to have your car or house key in your hand before you reach the car or apartment. Is there an added zap of energy to help keep you safe? Yes, indeed! Try this spell.

Supplies: A pin or nail; a white candle to help you focus; your two hands; the object you wish to protect.

Instructions: Heat the end of the pin or nail, then carve your name into the candle. Light the candle. Study the flame. Close your eyes and see the flame. If you cannot visualize, "feel" the flame. Keep practicing this exercise until you are comfortable. Once you are confident, hold your hands over the object you wish to protect, and say:

Too hot to touch!

Keep repeating these words as your hands grow warm over the object. Envision the heat and light of the candle going into the object, and making that object too hot to touch for anyone without permission. Make the sign of the pentacle (page 62) over the item with the candle. Allow the candle to burn completely.

To enhance this spell:

- Perform on a Sunday in the hour of the sun.

- Perform on a full moon.

- Renew once a month.

- Add a personal protective sigil on the item.

- Use on your car or truck.

- Keep a record of all expensive equipment, jewelry, etc. in your safety deposit box.

- Use on a new purse, wallet, or briefcase.

- Use on the front and back doors and windows, too, if you want to feel extra secure.

- Use on expensive jewelry, art collections, CDs, etc.

Spells for Travel and Trips

Most of us aren't sedentary people. We travel to and from work, we go shopping, and we take day trips, weekend trips, and long vacations. We visit our relatives, run errands, and if we have kids, become a veritable bus service. With all the tearing around that we do, we really need to think about our safety outside of the home.

Shopping with a Gargoyle

We all have to go shopping, whether it's for food, medicinal needs, or just for fun, but while we are shopping, we can be vulnerable. From bait-and-switch schemes to unknown creatures who slaver after our swinging purses (or back-pocket wallets), we can be a target.

Predators look for victims who seem unsure of themselves or who are not paying attention to what is going on around them. Learn to walk with confidence. That's where the gargoyle comes in. Gargoyles are man-made mythical beasts prominent in the Middle Ages, and the favored guardian for cathedrals (they also functioned as rain spouts).

You may wish to copy a picture or purchase a small statue of a gargoyle to help you visualize the first few times you try

this technique. Simply sit down, concentrate on your ever-friendly gargoyle, close your eyes, see it in your mind, and ask for its assistance in protection while you shop. As a fun experiment, shop without the gargoyle, then shop with the gargoyle, then again, shop without it. Keep a record of your experiences.

Other suggestions:

- Take your gargoyle with you on a camping trip.

- Take your gargoyle with you to your mother-in-law's house. Tell your gargoyle that your mother-in-law is dessert (just kidding!).

Practical Tip

Do use your common sense. Park your vehicle in a well-lighted area, and never, ever park next to a van with a sliding door. Don't swing your purse around like a shot put. During holiday shopping, make more than one trip to the car if you have a lot of packages and lock them out of view. Better yet, take a friend with you. Keep your eye on the people in front and behind you in the mall (use that peripheral vision Spirit gave you). Don't flash your cash.

Vacation Magick

Everybody wants to beat feet to that favorite vacation spot, but before you do that you need to ensure that the property you leave behind will be safe and secure (and there upon your return!). Inform your neighbors that you will be away. If you can get a housesitter, go for it. Have someone pick up your mail and other deliveries while you are gone. Stimulate that "somebody's home" idea by using lights on timers, along with a radio that will turn on and off by itself. Use the too hot to touch spell on page 49 on the front door of your home, then station your friendly gargoyle directly inside the front door. Ask a deceased relative (I'm not joking) who loved you very much to watch over your property while you are gone.

Ward your car (if you are traveling in your vehicle) with holy water and a circle of salt. (This is, of course, after you have taken it to the garage and they've done a thorough check for your safe travel.) Hang a piece of smoky quartz somewhere in the car to keep it from breaking down. (Now, if your car is put together with rubber bands and glue, don't expect the gem to keep it together.) Plan the most direct route to your destination. Do invest in a travel program that can tell you what roads or towns to avoid. Before you leave, put your hands over the map that marks your route and ask that Spirit guide you safely on your trip.

Hotel & Motel Magick

Supplies: Place a small piece of amethyst in every bag (especially if your bags are flying without you). Carry a small bag that contains the following items: Incense or sage; holy water; a piece of amethyst; a burning bowl; and a religious icon of your choice.

Instructions: Clear every room you stay in with the sage, holy water, or both. Set the religious icon where it is reflected by a mirror. (It is better if the icon is innocuous or very scary.) Once you have cleared the room, take a glass from the bathroom and fill it halfway with water. Ask that your ancestors protect the room and your belongings for the duration of your stay. Ask that the water soak up any negativity that enters the room. Before you leave, throw the water away and thank your ancestors. When you take a bath or shower, draw the rune Algiz (Υ) in the condensation on the mirror in the bathroom. This rune is associated with the Valkyries, female warriors of the Heathen Way who protect and guard you in life and after death. Algiz deflects negative influences from people and property. For extra protection, combine the runes Sol, Algiz, and Asa.

If You Get Lost

They are now installing "man finders" in cars—yes, those great little compasses that bob about on the ceiling close to the windshield. If your "man finder" poops out, here are a few mundane and magickal tips.

- Drive to a public place and check the map. Do not stop on the highway or along a dark or deserted street.

- Hold your hands over the map, and say, "Holy Mother, Goddess Divine, make my path clear, give me a sign." (She will.)

- You can also purchase the new satellite-driven Magellan System. With this new-fangled gadget, you won't ever be lost!

Practical Tip

Don't flash your cash. Don't rent a car at night. Keep a record of your traveler's check numbers and credit card numbers in a safe place. Take only the credit cards you plan to use. Never, ever tell strangers who you are, how much cash you are carrying, or where you plan to go. Determine the most direct route from your room to the fire escapes and elevators. Use all auxiliary locking devices. Never leave expensive items or cash in your hotel room. Arrange your things in the room so that you will know immediately if anything is amiss.

Web of Light

A Pagan police officer in Tennessee told me that when he was out in his patrol car, he would often conjure a web of light around himself if he got that "particularly hairy feeling" before he went into unusual situations. "I would also cast the web in front of the patrol car while I was driving to help me ferret out people in trouble. And you know, it worked every time!"

Airplane & Airport Magick

Statistically, you have a very slim chance of spiraling from the heavens and into a flaming pile on the face of Gaia—but that doesn't help the preflight (or in-flight) jitters for some. Here are some magickal tips for you frequent (or infrequent) fliers.

- Make sure each piece of luggage carries a small amethyst for protection. Empower the stone to meet you safely at your destination.

- Tag your bags with a black silk cord. Empower the cord to protect your baggage. You will also be able to discern your baggage from others much like it when you pick it up at the baggage claim.

- Pack as lightly as possible. The heavier the bags, the bigger the target you become.

- Expensive designer luggage or clothes draw unnecessary attention. Trust me, I've flown all over the United States. Jeans, tee shirts, sweatshirts, and sneakers are quite acceptable, help you to blend in with the masses, and keep you free of setting off the airport security alarms (since you have no reason to wear all that jewelry). If you must take that designer stuff, then do an invisibility spell, which is a simple form of visualization. See your luggage turning into various colors that blend into each other, and then the colors blending into the other luggage at the airport—sort of like a heat mirage. Don't get too good at this though, or you'll go to Kansas City and your luggage will land in Baltimore.

- Although you should lock your bags in the hotel room, don't bother on the airline. To search your bags, they will bust the locks or delay you at the baggage claim area while your bags are systematically searched. Instead, entreat Mercury, the god of travel and communication, to protect your belongings.

- As you step onto the plane, draw a banishing pentacle on the outside of the plane, asking for protection and banishing any negativity surrounding the plane. (I do it all the time. I don't care if the steward thinks I'm nuts.)

- If you are really nervous, say the following: "Dear guardian angel (or spirit guide). If there is something wrong with this plane, please don't let them board us." Three times in the last five years I have made this request, and three times they have had to make major repairs and didn't let us board. In one case we took an entirely different plane.

- If you start to panic during the flight, close your eyes, count down from ten to one, and repeat a positive affirmation. Be sure to check that it is your panic you are feeling. Planes are enclosed places with lots of people. The man three seats behind you could be in a frenzied spiral, and it is his energy you are feeling—not your own emotions. If you feel uncomfortable, look around you. I'd bet my broomstick someone else is feeding your fear.

Protecting Your Vehicle

With the rising costs of owning, maintaining, and insuring a vehicle these days, it is a definite financial setback if something happens to your car, and even more of a catastrophe if you happen to be in it when the rubber of a tractor trailer hits the roof of your vehicle rather than on the pavement it belongs. This spell is designed to ward your car from damages and keep you safe. I can't swear in a court of law that it will stop accidents from happening, but my family feels that it has certainly helped, and my daughter will tell you honestly that she thinks this particular spell saved her life when she was involved in a bad accident.

In this spell, we call on the power of the goddess Hecate. Hecate, the Grecian, pre-Hellenic goddess of the moon, night, magick, wealth, education, knowledge, and ceremony is the goddess of the crossroads. In this position she is called Hecate Trevia, Hecate of the Three Ways. During the Middle Ages, Hecate was called the Queen of Ghostworld. German worshippers knew her as Dame Holda, Queen of the Ghostways. Hecate has the power to avert physical and financial storms and her mythos entwines with several triads, including Hecate, Diana, and Lucina; and Hecate, Persephone, and Demeter. You may wish to entreat her assistance when dumping the dirt at the crossroads. Hecate was later identified as a form of Artemis. Although Middle Age sources lend Hecate's magick to wicked intent, she is truly the Goddess of Great Mystery, embodying the dark side of ourselves that we much reach to obtain wholeness. Therefore, she did not stand for evil, but for the mystery that these writers could not comprehend.

Supplies: A small bottle of blessed spring water; 3 cups pickling salt, sea salt, or table salt.

Instructions: On a full moon, take the spring water and, with your finger, draw a pentacle on the following:

- All windows.

- All doors.

- All tires.

- On the hood.

- On the trunk (back hatch, or bed of truck).

- On the roof.

Pentacle

Say:

> Great Mother, Hecate, I call ye forth.
> Gracious Goddess up above,
> protect herein all I love.
> Keep them safe and free from harm,
> if not be right, set off alarm.
> Transport us safely from here to there,
> let no weather be a care.
> My car (truck) turns right,
> my car (truck) turns left,
> keep it free from harm or theft.
> Circle of protection gather round,
> when danger comes hunting
> we can't be found.

Sprinkle the pickling salt in a clockwise direction on the street around the vehicle. Try to keep an unbroken line. Say:

> This spell is sealed. This spell is locked.
> All negative energy is thoroughly blocked.

To enhance this spell:

- Place a piece of empowered smoky quartz on the dash or in the glove compartment to ward off mechanical failures.

- Place a bag of protective herbs inside the car to ward off negativity or theft.

- Perform on a full moon or when the moon is in Mercury (as Mercury governs transportation).

If Your Car Breaks Down

I was originally taught this spell for healing unknown maladies of the body, and you'll find it for that purpose in my book *American Folk Magick: Charms, Spells, and Herbals*. However, I've had more than one magickal practitioner who has told me that this verbal chant works well for sick and broken cars. Hey, it can't hurt to try!

Instructions: Hold your hands over the hood of the vehicle and recite the following verse three times:

And these signs shall follow those
that believeth in Spirit.
They shall cast out demons,
and they shall speak in new tongues.
And if they drink anything deadly,
it shall not harm them.
They shall lay hands upon the sick,
and they shall recover,
In the name of Spirit, so mote it be!

Tap the hood of the car three times with your fingers. Seal the spell by using your index finger to draw an equal-armed cross over the hood of the car.

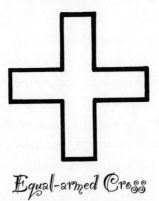

Equal-armed Cross

Protection Spells for Your Home

We'd like to think we are always secure in our homes, but if that was so, then there wouldn't be any such thing as burglary (or worse). A house blessing and protection ritual can be as complicated or as simple as you like, but usually incorporate the use of the four elements (earth, air, fire, and water) and the request that Spirit guide the energies in and outside of the home.

Bless Your House

Choose the deity that most represents your feelings about the divine. For this particular spell, I've used Brigid, Celtic (Irish) goddess of water and fire, whose healing energies will help to cleanse a home where the environment has been punctured by abuse, harsh arguments, or other negative manifestations. Her festival is one of the four great feasts of the Celtic religion, held on February 1 (Candlemas). The totem for this goddess is the cow, and offerings of milk are acceptable. Carry the four elements around your house, imagining that all negativity is banished from each room.

When finished, stand in the center of the room, and say:

> I am the wind on the sea.
> I am a wave of the ocean.
> I am the roar of the sea.
> I am a powerful ox.
> I am a hawk on a cliff.
> I am a dewdrop in sunshine.
> I am the strength of art.
> I am a spear with spoils that wages battle.
> I have cleared the stony place upon the mountain.[9]
> From basement to attic. From sill to door.
> From roof to landscaping. I fill this house
> with the protective energy of (name deity)
> and ask for blessings upon each person
> who resides here. So mote it be!

Renew every six months. This ancient Celtic poem magickally declares your sovereignty over your home.

----

9. Marie-Luise Sjoestedt, *Gods and Heroes of the Celts,* "Amairgin's Song (Historical)" (Berkeley, CA: Turtle Island Foundation), p. 23.

To enhance this spell:

- Perform on a full moon.

- Perform on Monday (family matters) or Sunday (success).

- Perform when the moon is in Cancer or Virgo.

- Perform in the hour of the moon.

- Perform yearly on February 1.

- Perform on New Year's Day.

The Morrigan Protection Incense for the Home[10]

Supplies: ¼ cup coarsely ground cedar shavings; ½ tablespoon finely ground dragon's blood resin; 15 drops musk oil; 11 drops patchouli oil; ½ tablespoon crushed lavender buds; ¼ teaspoon crushed mugwort.

Instructions: Best made at the dark of the moon. Start with cedar shavings, adding ingredients in order given. Mix well after each addition. Concentrate on the protective energy of the Morrigan while mixing. Store in a jar or plastic bag. Add to charcoal to burn. As the incense burns, hold your hands over the smoke, and say:

**From Spirit to herb, from herb to incense,
from incense to flame, from flame to smoke,
from smoke to Spirit, I empower this incense
in the name of *(pick deity)*
for the purpose of *(state intent)*.**

---

10. Created by Morgana of Morgana's Chamber.

Florida Water

Florida water recipes are magickal washes for floors in homes or businesses, and are primarily used for ridding the environment of negativity and evil. You can also use these washes to cleanse magickal tools, or put in a spray bottle for quickie cleansings.

Supplies: ½ gallon of 90 proof alcohol; 1 pint spring water; 1 tablespoon squeezed lemon juice; 10 drops protection oil.

Instructions: Mix during a full moon, though anytime will do, especially if you feel you have an emergency.

Practical Tip

Have you run a safety check on your home or apartment lately? Have you secured your doors with good quality single or double-cylinder locks? Do you have a door viewer (peephole)? Have you replaced hollow-core doors with solid-core doors? Taken special precautions with a sliding glass door or sliding windows? (Hint: use a broomstick.) Do you have adequate interior and exterior lighting? Have you trimmed your shrubbery so a criminal cannot find easy concealment? Padlocked exterior electrical boxes to prevent someone from cutting your power?

Folk Charms for House & Apartment Protection

Here is a great list of quickie protection charms I've collected over the years.

- Cut an onion in half and set both halves on the windowsill in the kitchen. Empower to suck up negativity. Change when the onion sprouts.

- Hang a pair of open scissors over the front door to cut off negativity from entering the house.

- Put garlic under the bed to ward off nightmares.

- Scent your pillow with lavender to bring sweet dreams.

- Place Penelope's web (page 47) over the mouth of a Mason jar filled with broken glass. This is to trap unwanted nasties and cut them to smithereens!

- Place holy water by the left side (as you face it) of the front door.

- Make a prayer monument built of small, round, white stones in one corner of your property. A small pile will do. Leave milk and honey for the spirits of the property and entreat their protection.

- Place a small bag of angelica, rosemary, and mint under the four eaves of the attic (or on the four corners of the property).

- To stave off a coming storm, stick a knife in the ground, blade pointing in the direction of the oncoming nasty weather to split the wind. Scream, "I am the presence!" at the top of your lungs, directed at the oncoming storm. (You think I jest? It worked for me!)

- Hang a cluster of acorns on the front door to protect the residence and those who live there.

- Place a full glass of water by your bed every night to collect any negativity in the room. (No, you can't put your teeth in there!)

- Put a mothball in each corner of the room to absorb negativity. (And if you put them around your trash outside, the critters won't rip open your garbage.)

- If you can help it, don't make a major housing move when the moon is void of course, or when Mercury, Jupiter, or Venus are retrograde.

Practical Tip

There's crime in rural areas, too. Be a good neighbor and keep your eyes open. Use your locks. Just because you made it out of the sweltering city doesn't mean that criminals aren't lurking. Keep locks, gates, and fences in good repair. Secure access roads, equipment, outbuildings, and livestock. (Use Pennsylvania Dutch hex signs—they work!) Store harvested crops in protected areas. Post your property. Use outdoor lighting with automatic timers.

Fruity Vibrations

Exotic incenses too much of a pain to make? Can't afford good, prepackaged incense? Dried, thinly sliced, or crushed fruit skins can clear out any room in your home and increase the positive vibrations. You can place the shavings on a charcoal brick (made especially for incense) or simply put them in a little pile and burn them with your lighter.

Orange peel: Harmony and positive production

Lemon peel: Clarification and stimulation

Apple peel: Love and healing

Not allowed to burn stuff? (Hey, sometimes you can't.) Add to a pot of boiling water, throw in a little silk bag, or scatter in the corners of a room. You'll get the same results.

Evening Prayer

In Pennsylvania Dutch Country (my neck of the woods), it is appropriate to request a blessing of the home and property as you make your last rounds before retiring. You are to repeat the following prayer three times:

My house has four corners
One, two, three, four.
Four holy angels adorn them
From rafter to core.

Neither criminals, nor charmers
Above or below.
Nor those who do evil
Can enter my home.

My house has four corners
One, two, three, four.
Four holy angels adorn them
Protected to the core.

My home stands with Spirit
Encompassed by love.
Protected from evil
And blessed by the dove.

My house has four corners
One, two, three, four.
Surrounded by angels
Infused by Spirit
From present to future.
So mote it be!

This is a great prayer to teach your children. You can also anoint the four corners of your home with protection oil while repeating the prayer.

Protecting Those in the Home

Handkerchief Spell

My great-grandfather was a tent revivalist first in West Virginia, and then in Pennsylvania. When I was a little girl, my grandmother would purchase white handkerchiefs (for the men) and embroidered ones (for the ladies) and then take them to her weekly ladies' prayer circle. In the heyday of her father's spiritual pursuits it was common practice to place said handkerchiefs on the altar, and either the minister would imbue them with healing and protective energy or the congregation as a whole would pray over the pieces of cloth. Sometimes, photographs of those requesting protection or healings would be placed on a specific handkerchief (that was in later years when the camera/photo were more easily obtained).

Supplies: A white handkerchief for each member of the family; blessed spring water; sea salt or table salt; your choice of protection incense; an individual picture of each member of the family.

Instructions: Lay the handkerchiefs on a flat surface. Make sure they are opened, not folded. Sprinkle each one with the spring water and sea salt, envisioning the pieces of cloth glowing with purity. Pass the handkerchief over the incense three times. Place a photo on each piece of cloth. (Remember what handkerchief belongs to whom.) Hold your hands over the first picture, and say:

And Spirit wrought special miracles from the hands of the children of the Gods, so that from their hands were brought unto the sick or fearful pieces of cloth or aprons, and the diseases departed from them, and the evil spirits went out of them.[11]

Take your time and envision pure, white light entering your body from the crown chakra and moving down through your heart, out your arms, into your hands, and into the photo and handkerchief. When you lose your concentration, or feel that you are finished, take a deep breath and seal the magick by making the sign of the

---

11. The original version is from the Bible, Acts 11, 12.

equal-armed cross (page 65) over the photo and the handkerchief. Go on to the next piece of cloth. When you are finished, thank Spirit for your work this day. Give the handkerchief to the appropriate person to carry with them. Renew every six months, or before if you feel it is necessary.

To enhance this spell:

- Add a mixture of personally chosen protective herbs to the sea salt.

- Perform on the full moon.

- Perform on a Monday in the hour of the moon.

- Perform on the individual's birthday.

- Empower in the name of a specific divinity.

- Give to a sick friend.

- Tuck into an ailing pet's collar.

- Give to your favorite police officer, EMT driver, fireman, or military service personnel.

Protection Against Pregnancy[12]

In the 1960s, Dr. Eugene Jonas, a Czechoslovakian gynecologist, discovered a method of family planning that had actually been used for centuries by European women. He determined that a woman is at the peak of her fertility at the time of the month when the moon is in the same phase in which she was born. Therefore, if you were born during a first quarter moon, then for the three days surrounding that same moon phase (given that you are a woman), you will be the most fertile of any days in your current cycle. Of course, this information will work quite well for you if you are trying to have a baby, and if you're not, then stay away from those passionate moments during the three days surrounding your original moon-birth phase. How do you find out what phase the moon was in when you were born? Many astrological charts will give you this information.

----

12. Lori Reid, *Moon Magick* (New York: Three Rivers Press, Crown Publishers, 1988).

Preventing Barrenness

The Pennsylvania Dutch, of Old World German extraction, had a compendium of folk magickal practices that, if you dig deep enough, you can find and put to modern use. Easter egg coloring and decoration have been widely practiced in the Dutchified areas since the 1800s. To prevent barrenness, each family would decorate dozens of eggs with cheerful, unique patterns. Then the eggs were hung on a birch or cherry tree whose trunk and limbs were wrapped in cotton batting. The egg, seen as an ancient fertility symbol, brings the same energies in sympathy of the woman of the household, and she is responsible for hanging the eggs and asking for the blessing of deity with the tying of the ribbon suspending each egg. If you don't want to go to all the work of blowing out each egg and then decorating that delicate shell, you can always purchase those colorful plastic eggs that are so abundant around Easter, insert various symbols of fertility in each egg, then hang them on a miniature tree dedicated to the spirit of fertility.

For Your Friends and Social Situations

Interacting with others outside the family can be just as important to your emotional well-being as associating with your blood relatives. The following rituals and spells were designed especially for your friends.

Wolf Protection Ritual[13]

Our country is rich with Native American heritage that many of us have been unable to tap. This ritual was sent to me by Dream Wolfdancer and works well by yourself, or within a group or coven environment, or just for your family.

Supplies: Fire pit, old grill, or cauldron; the means to make a fire; sage.

Instructions: Make the fire. Light. Say:

> Hiya . . . hiya . . . hiya . . . hekohey!
> On this night, from the forest and field,
> den and dark, I call you, great wolf!

----

13. Copyright ©1998 Dream Wolfdancer.

Clap your hands or beat a drum in rhythm like a heartbeat as you say:

Mother, mother, nursing your pups,
Watch over me and mine.
Father, father, protecting your family,
Watch over me and mine.
Come O sisters and brothers of the clan!
Come dance in the firelight!
Feast on the bounty of the hunt!
Sing with us in the dark!
And hunt within our dreams.
Owooooooooooooo! Owooooooooooooo!

Burn the sage and spread smoke over each friend or family member. Pick up dry earth and sprinkle over the flames, saying:

We are one!

Visualize an alpha pair playing with their pups. Say:

My clan is safe. Many thanks, brother wolf.

Leave an offering for Father Sky and Mother Earth.

The Charm String

Popular in the Ozark Mountains in the early 1900s, the charm string consists of buttons and good wishes from your friends, and is used to ward off negativity and bring you good fortune. The charm string was not only considered lucky, but became a beloved memory book for women who could not read. A button from someone's birthday party, a wedding, christening, first date, etc., was thought to be extra special.

Supplies: Collect a button from each of your friends, asking them to bless it with protection and love.

Instructions: String them together, asking deity for protection, love, and luck. Use the charm string for all sorts of protection magick, or carry it in your purse or briefcase to bring continuous good fortune and protection. If you are having a particularly bad day, arrange the charm string in a circle around your picture.

To enhance this spell:

- Make on a Friday in the hour of Venus.

- Make on the full moon.

- Make when the moon is in Leo.

Collect buttons from your friends for:

- A friend who is sick.

- A friend who is moving away.

- A child going off to college.

Sexual Assault Prevention (SAP) Spell

Don't be fooled by what anyone tells you—rape is definitely about control, power, and anger. Rape is an act of violence—an attempt to control and degrade you by using sex as a weapon. Rape can happen to anyone and the attacker can be anyone. There is no delineation between the type of victim or the type of attacker.

This simple little spell finds its roots in Pennsylvania Dutch Pow-Wow magick and was used to ward off negativity of all types.

Supplies: 1 large safety pin.

Instructions: Hold the pin in both hands, and say:

> **Blood and bone**
> **Wall like stone**
> **Protect me by my Lady's throne.**
> **Edge of pin**
> **Strike at them**
> **Hit your mark like a javelin.**

Envision yourself surrounded by a protective, white light. Move the light into the pin. Keep chanting the above charm until the pin grows very hot in your hand. Then hold the pin over your head, and say:

> **It is done!**

Wear the pin on the left sleeve of your shirt, blouse, jacket, or dress. Re-empower once a month.

To enhance this spell:

• Perform on a Saturday.

• Perform on the dark of the moon.

• Perform on Tuesday in the hour of Saturn.

• Perform when the moon is in Scorpio or Leo.

- Add black beads to the pin and give to a dear friend before they go on vacation or a business trip.

- Bless the pin with the energy of a protective god or goddess.

- Add extra punch with your choice of protection oil (though wipe thoroughly before you slip that pin onto your favorite silk blouse). **Note:** Some women prefer to wear the pin over their heart, pinned to the bra.

Practical Tip

Be smart! Walk with confidence and purpose wherever you go. Always be aware of your surroundings. Don't let drugs or alcohol screw up your thinking process. Travel with a friend if you must go to strange places or parties thrown by people you don't know. If your Internal Warning System is beeping like crazy—listen to it! Avoid date rape. Know your intentions. Say what you mean and mean what you say. If you don't know your date well, always drive your own vehicle.

Protecting the Servant Who Protects You

Police officers in our country have an especially difficult job. As our population increases, so does our crime rate. When your law enforcement spouse or partner leaves the protection of your environment, they face far more negative energies than most ordinary people. Here's a spell to help keep them safe and alleviate some of your worries. And what better symbol to use in our spell than the star, probably discovered as a result of astronomical research in the Euphrates-Tigris region about 6,000 years ago, and used today for various law enforcement agencies as well as the American military.

The points of the star (or pentacle) have two meanings—earth, air, water, fire, and the Spirit of man (enclosed in a circle adds the Universal Spirit); and the arms, legs, and head of the human body. In 400 B.C. Pythagoreans used the sign widely and added it to the bottom of any missive to send a wish of good health. The star was the official seal of the city of Jerusalem during 300–150 B.C. We can also find the pentacle in pre-Columbian America through the Mayan culture.

Some historians believe that the pentacle is based on the symbol of the goddess Kore (Grecian), although she is also identified with the Roman goddess Libera. Clement of Alexandria, in a Christianized version, celebrated her worship on January 5 as the Eve of Epiphany of Kore. Finally, the pentacle signifies one's oath (apropos here with the oath of an individual in law enforcement).

The pentacle (star) used as a protective symbol is the sign of the Roman Venus, goddess of fertility and war. Other goddesses associated with the pentacle are Ishtar, Astarte, Kore, Nephthys, and Isis. (Does your mother belong to the Order of the Eastern Star? Now you know where the symbolism really comes from.)

Venus, with her love of order and beauty is a perfect choice when petitioning for protection of your loved one. Her festival, the Vinalia, was celebrated on April 23. Venus was once a Lady of Animals, and her horned consort, Adonis, was both hunter and sacrificial stag. The word "veneration" has its root in Venus. Although modern historians often equate Venus to sex and the pleasures thereof, she is a powerful protective Goddess and cares deeply about those who petition her for assistance.

Supplies: A white candle; a needle or nail; ground mistletoe (if you don't have mistletoe, choose another protective herb from the appendix); a pentacle (page 62) drawn on a white piece of paper; a picture of your loved one; his or her law enforcement badge; holy water (water mixed with three pinches of salt and empowered to Spirit).

Instructions: Inscribe the pentacle, point up, on the white candle with a needle or nail, then inscribe the symbol of Venus (♀) over the pentacle. Rub with crushed mistletoe (if you have used the berries, do not put your fingers in your mouth before washing thoroughly). Place the paper with the pentacle (point side up) on your altar or working surface. Set the candle at the top point of the pentacle. Put the picture of your loved one in the center of the pentacle. Place the badge on top of the picture. Sprinkle the badge with holy water, visualizing white light and protection around the shield and the picture. Light the white candle. Hold your arms in the air so that your body becomes a star. Say:

I call forth the energies of Venus to protect you
every hour and every minute of every day.
You have the strength of the ocean waves.
Ho. (*Touch the badge, visualizing this gift pouring
into the badge and into your loved one.*)
You have the protective love of your family
Ho. (*Repeat touching the badge.*)
You walk surely upon the stability of Mother Earth.
Ho. (*Repeat touching the badge.*)
The winds of wisdom touch your mind.
Ho. (*Repeat touching the badge.*)
You carry the protective fire within you.
Ho. (*Repeat touching the badge.*)
You have the strength of the ocean waves.
Ho. (*Repeat touching the badge.*)
The earth, the sky, the sea lend their
protection to you.
Ho. (*Repeat touching the badge.*)
As I will, so mote it be!
Ho. (*Repeat touching the badge.*)

Make the sign of the pentacle on yourself. Do this by touching the left breast, the forehead, the right breast, the left shoulder, the right shoulder, and back to the left breast. Return the badge to its owner. Let the candle burn completely. **Note:** If your spouse or partner can do this ritual with you, your spell will have twice the impact.

To enhance this spell:

- Do on Friday, the day of Venus.

- Do in the hour of Venus.

- Do on a Saturday (banishing) in the hour of Venus.

- Do under the full moon (more power).

- Do under the dark moon (banishing negativity).

Practical Tip

How street smart are you? Do you jog or walk alone on deserted streets late at night? Do you leave your purse in the grocery basket while you run back down the aisle to get something you forgot? Do you stuff money in your pockets in a big wad? Do you leave your wallet in your suit coat, then hang it on a coat rack? Do you tell people on the Internet your telephone number or address? Do you leave your car unlocked because you'll be back in a few minutes? If you answered "yes" to any of these questions, you need an attitude adjustment on your personal safety!

Preventative Magick—Moon in the Signs

Each month the moon travels through all twelve signs of the zodiac, spending about two and a half days in each sign. And yes, you're going to need some sort of astrological almanac to use this kind of magick.

- Use moon in Aries for protecting a new venture, quick results, rescuing people, courage, and conflict. Natural ruler is Mars, whose energies best relate to action.

- Use moon in Taurus for protecting money, art, kids, pregnancy, and ethics. Natural ruler is Venus. Venus concerns herself with cash money, your stuff, beauty, the arts, and lust. She's not the marrying kind—for that type of energy, choose the asteroid Juno.

- Use the moon in Gemini for protecting or enhancing communication, short-distance travel, and siblings. Natural ruler is Mercury, best known for wit, quick thinking, and communication.

- Use moon in Cancer for protecting your home, real estate, past actions, traditions, graves, the garden, and your integrity. Natural ruler is the moon, which relates primarily to our emotions and family matters.

- Use the moon in Virgo to protect your health, workplace, hunters, computer, pets, the earth, the coven, or people in the armed service or police. Natural ruler is Mercury.

- Use the moon in Libra to protect a partnership, negotiation, justice, social functions, friends, and jewelry. Natural ruler is Venus.

- Use the moon in Scorpio to protect your willpower, soulmate, occult work, yourself during surgery, insurance claims, ritual functions, taxes, and integrity. Natural ruler is Pluto, the planet of regeneration.

- Use the moon in Sagittarius to protect religion, philosophy, law, long trips, parties, sports, future goals, your sense of humor, and publishing. Natural ruler is Jupiter, the planet of expansion.

- Use the moon in Capricorn to protect your career, your honor, a promotion, your social standing, long-term finances, and wisdom. Natural ruler is Saturn. Saturn's energies are orderly, diligent, and constrictive. Use caution when working with Saturn.

- Use the moon in Aquarius to protect your friends, peers, luck, clubs, the future in general, electrical appliances, coven workings, and your own honesty. Natural ruler is Uranus, which is the liberator of the zodiac.

- Use the moon in Pisces for protecting your dreams, from getting swindled, the stuff you plant, your spirituality, and dark, scary secrets. Natural ruler is Neptune.

Now that I gave you all this great information, what are you supposed to do with it? Get out your astrological planner and look at the above list. Is there anything on there you would like to protect short-term? Find the corresponding moon-in-sign entry in your little book and circle that date(s). Write a note to yourself like this:

October 16—Moon in Aquarius—Burn a black candle to ward off negativity from Geraldine.

Simple? Yes. Effective? Absolutely!

Okay, so not all things will fall into place with the moon in the signs—life is unpredictable. There's no reason, though, why you can't learn what the moon in the signs means, and plan your magick accordingly. Once you begin using this type of magick, you'll wonder how you did without it for so long!

Lunar Eclipse
General Protection Ritual

According to our astrology friends, the eclipse is an interesting heavenly phenomenon that, if used magickally, can give us a real positive kick where we need it the most. The effects of a lunar eclipse can be felt from one week before it up to six months afterwards, though some astrologers argue the point and tell us that a lunar eclipse's strongest effect is from the day before to approximately thirty days after. You'll have to do your own experimentation to clear up that point for yourself. The astrological house that the eclipse occurs in will give you a clue to fine-tuning your magick. What sign the moon is in will also help you to prepare your choices of correspondences (herbs, candle colors, etc.), and the moon phase can lead you toward banishing or manifesting energies. If it is a full moon, you are in luck—the magick can go either way. Finally, if you really want to tweak that magick an extra pinch, have an astrologer tell you where, in your transit chart, the eclipse will hit and what planets it will talk to (or not) in your natal chart. If you don't want to get that investigative about the whole thing, that's fine, too.

Each lunar eclipse has a beginning, middle, and end.
Again, astrologers differ on the topic of timing. Some feel
that in order to capture the heavenly energies in your net of
magick, you should do the ritual before the beginning of the
astrological occurrence. Others aren't so meticulous. In the
example here, I readied my supplies and empowered my candles and incense before the actual eclipse. This took approximately one hour of my time, as I had many issues to cover.
Then I did a preliminary outdoor ritual at the beginning of
the eclipse and made an offering of milk, honey, and incense
to deity. This involved approximately fifteen minutes of my
time. At the midpoint of the eclipse (the
time the almanacs tell you) I drew the
energies into the ritual. Finally, at the
end of the eclipse, I sealed all the energies
I worked with that day or evening.

Before the ritual I sat down with three-
by-five-inch cards and thought carefully
about how I wanted to use the energies of
the lunar eclipse. The moon was in Leo,
and it was full—two extra boosts of energy.

I decided that I wanted to protect my finances, my career, my home, and my magickal group. Granted, there were other things I could have done with this eclipse (and did), but right now, we are focusing on the issue of protection. I wrote down my specific desires on three-by-five-inch cards separated by topic. On the last card, I wrote the word "Success." I chose four seven-day candles (red, black, green, and purple) and one taper candle (yellow)—red for moving things along, black for protecting my interests, green for healing over the next six months, and purple to enhance my spirituality. The last candle, the taper, was placed in the center of the table. This was my success candle, used to tie the energies of the other candles together.

On the red and green candles I drew the symbol for Jupiter (expansive energy), Mercury (easy flow), and Venus (universal love). On the black candle I carved the banishing pentagram (to banish negativity). On all the candles I carved the astrological symbol for the moon and for Leo, as the moon was in Leo. I empowered all the symbols with magickal oil. I then mixed various herbs and incenses for two purposes:

one mixture was for the ritual itself, the second mixture was focused primarily on protection. I used the base incenses in this book and added cinquefoil (because I had two court cases running); elder leaves (to break especially nasty negative energies); and yellow dock (to increase financial prosperity). Then I sprinkled a bit of the first incense on the top of each candle. Finally, I put my three-by-five-inch cards under the matching candles so that when I was performing the ritual, I would remember the energies that I had chosen to work on.

A few minutes before the start of the eclipse, I walked outside with a glass of milk, a piece of bread with honey, my protection incense and charcoal, and a bag of Morgana's protection powder. With the moon in full view, I went to place the milk and bread on my outside altar, only to discover that my father had put my outside altar in the shed because of the freezing weather. So much for that. Instead, I put the milk and bread on the ground where the altar normally is, silently offering these things to divinity. I then lit the charcoal and waited for the incense to catch. Very slowly, I held up the bowl so that I could see the moon over the rim, ensconced in the smoke from the incense.

As I said my prayers, I went into the alpha state and the moon split in two, providing me with the sacred Eyes of the Night. As I finished my prayers and came out of the alpha state, the two orbs joined and became whole.

At this point I walked clockwise around my property, scattering the protection powder. I made sure to hit our vehicles, each side of the house, and all the doors with the protection powder. I then went back to my original station, thanked deity, and piled more incense on the charcoal. I left the charcoal burning in the dish on a large, flat stone. Part one of the ritual was now completed.

Part two of the ritual involved casting a circle of protection, invoking deity, additional empowerment of the candles, and lighting them, followed by a period of raising energy and meditation. As I re-empowered and prayed over each candle, I remained focused on what was written on my three-by-five-inch cards. Finally, I released the circle, putting the energy back into the candles.

Part three was performed precisely at the time that the eclipse was astrologically considered "over." I prayed once more, with my palms facing the lit candles, then walked clockwise around the outside of the house, again asking for protection. This time, I scattered sea salt to form a final barrier against negativity.

The above ritual is considered a basic, spontaneous ritual because I didn't work or speak with a script. Instead, I used my intuition. I began the ritual when it felt right, and I said what I felt was most appropriate. As I had no anger in my heart, the ritual went smoothly. The time for anger at various circumstances that lead to my actual performance of the ritual was over, and I worked with future preventative protective energies in mind. If some of you are screwing up your eyeballs thinking that this ritual is just too complicated, don't worry about it. Eventually, you might like to try something a little more intense and you need only turn to this ritual as your guide.

3

Banishing Those Lesser Irritations

When footsteps come

Within the night

And you're beset

By doubt and fright

Hold fast within

That darkest hour

For to the Witch

Her fear is power.

—David Norris ©1998

Big hurts and small hurts come our way. It would be silly to do a spell for every little thing that doesn't meet our expectations; however, we don't want to be a bunny in the headlights when that tractor-trailer of doom rushes to pulverize us into the macadam. Don't let the simple spells in this chapter fool you. Complicated procedures do not promise a successful working or indicate you are an accomplished magickal person. A snap of your fingers can literally keep the dogs from gnawing off your right toe—as long as you keep the following in mind:

- Don't panic.

- Assess the situation.

- Take action.

- Never target the innocent.

Practical Tip

All the spells in this chapter (and the next) are designed to turn away negative influences, stop attacks, and defend yourself. They are not to be used to begin an attack on an innocent individual. If you do, you're the one who's going to get thwapped. With every ritual you perform to send back negativity to the owner (especially if you must specify), it is necessary to:

- Do a personal cleansing.

- Do a healing rite or spell for the person who has experienced the injustice in conjunction with your call for justice.

Try to say a positive affirmation after each spell, and light a white candle while you request continued healing.

Simple Folk Spells for Little Troubles

The level of magick you use should match the seriousness of the problem. It's silly to do a full-blown ritual over a minor altercation that could best be handled by common sense or a few well-placed words. If you feel magick is necessary, but you aren't ready to pull out a complete altar setup or perform a three-hour drumming ceremony, then here are some very simple solutions for little troubles.

- Turn your shirt inside-out and slam it in a door to send back gossip. Light a white candle, and say: "Lift me above the sea of unkind words, Great Mother. Bring to me peace, harmony, and good will."

- Take your measure (head to toe) with red yarn and burn it to relieve yourself of the negativity that can build over a particularly stressful time. Light a white candle, and say: "Cleanse me of all negativity, Lord and Lady. Allow me to go forward in truth, honesty, and joy."

- Fill a cup with dirt and set it in the corner of the most traveled room in your house. Hold your hands over the cup and ask the element of earth to remove the negativity from your home (or life). Let set for seven days. Throw the dirt out.

• Write the name of the offending party on a piece of paper and put it in the freezer. Light a white candle, and say: "I have great power within me. Lord and Lady, bless and keep me in my hour of need."

• Cleanse your house with sage after a minor argument. Light a white candle, and say: "Fill my heart, my soul, my mind, and my home, Great Mother, with peace, tranquility, and love."

• Write the offending party's name on the ace of spades. Put it in an envelope and address it to the worst place on the planet. Light a white candle, and say: "Break the curse of negative words and actions that use me as a target, and fracture them like shattered glass upon the road. Grace me, Lord and Lady, with your divine intervention. I am confident, strong, and filled with power."

- Put the offending party's name in a pickle jar. Pour vinegar over the name. Close tight. Let them stew in their own juices. Light a white candle, and say: "Let this disruption upon me cease and desist, Lord and Lady. I am a strong and powerful individual."

- To break a minor hex, urinate on a brick and place it outside, beside your front door or stoop. (Too yucky for you? Hey, it works.) Light a white candle, and say: "Break the evil energy with a sizzle and a flame. No one can affect or detain me from an honorable purpose."

- To turn back psychic attack, play country music. Light a white candle, and say: "Go forth, legions of angels, and protect me. I am blessed with common sense."

- Write the word "justice" in the footprint of someone who has harmed you. Light a white candle, and say: "Assist me, Great Father, in my hour of need. May justice trip the person who has harmed me. Wise justice will prevail."

- Here's a nineties one. Make sure that the shadow of the person who has done you wrong falls on a sticky note.

Throw the note down the hole of a toilet. Light a white candle, and say: "The shadow of the self is the self. I banish (person's name) from my life. Water wash and water flow, (name of person) will go, go, go. I walk each day renewed in the light of universal harmony."

- Banish negative influences by writing them on a piece of toilet paper. Throw in the toilet. Add cleanser. Flush. Light a white candle, and say: "I deactivate any negativity with water and soap. The evil sinks like a flooded boat. I arise from this tempest strong and true."

- Write the problem on a piece of paper, tear it into threes, then throw it in the center of a crossroad. Ask the goddess Hecate to take the problem away. Then light a white candle, and say: "Mother Dark and sweet divine, Queen of Night, see my sign. Dominate that wretched swine. I will overcome all obstacles in my path, and be better for it."

- Mix a lock of your hair with elder leaves, then place in your palm, carry outside, and blow the hair and leaves off of your hand, saying: "What was bound, is now unbound."

- Cut a lemon in half. Take a shower. Rinse with the lemon juice to remove all negativity, then rinse with clear water. (This is an excellent morning pick-me-up any time, but especially when you are feeling depressed.) Light a white candle, and say, "Lemon light and cleansing might, remove all negativity from my mind, body, and soul. Free me from all evil. I meet the day with confidence and personal power."

- Put a birthday candle in a cup of dirt, light it, put it out, and break it. Throw the burned half away. Relight the remaining candle, and say: "All negativity around me is broken. I am filled with the loving light of the universe." When the candle is finished burning, throw the dirt out.

- Your store not doing so good? Crush onion and garlic skins into a fine powder. Add a pinch of brown sugar. Burn on a piece of charcoal to break up negativity in your place of business. Then, place one chestnut near the cash register. This will work for one month.

Eliminate Stress

When we find ourselves in the center of a negative situation or crisis, we tend to make more out of the small stuff than is necessary. Here are some quick ideas to help you relax and eliminate stress.

- Cleanse your home or apartment with burning sage and holy water.

- Don't forget your spiritual bath or shower.

- Do your spiritual devotions daily.[1]

- Burn a black candle to turn back negativity, then burn a white, blue, or purple candle to produce spiritual harmony.

- Boil basil in a small pot on the stove.

----

1. For more information on daily devotions, see my book *To Stir a Magick Cauldron* (Llewellyn, 1995).

- Sprinkle the corners of your basement and attic with a mixture of crushed angelica, rosemary, and basil (all herbs that you can get from the grocery store).

- Set aside at least five minutes each day to meditate. Visualize peace, prosperity, and joy entering your home. I use a calm scene, such as a pristine white beach and gentle, lapping waves.

All these things seem pretty easy, don't they? They may not even seem worth your time because they are so simple, but don't let the lack of embellishment fool you.

Practical Tip

Double-action candles (candles of two colors) work well for combination magick. Usually the top half is one color and the bottom half black. Double-action candles are difficult to obtain in many areas of the country. To solve this little dilemma, just put one votive candle on top of another. If you don't have a black votive (again, they may be hard to obtain out of season), use a brown one. Use the following rule of thumb:

Green and black (brown)—Success, luck, and money problems

Red and black—Love, sexual, or personal energy problems

White and black—Personal, business, or house cleansing

Crossed Conditions

A crossed condition is when the energy around you has somehow gone amuck, and rather than harmony, you are experiencing all sorts of setbacks, negative circumstances, or an unbelievable run of strange occurrences. Before you panic and think that someone has cursed you, remember that a crossed condition may be occurring because:

- You didn't listen to your instincts and plowed blindly ahead.

- You didn't listen to Spirit, who was urging you in a different direction.

- You may have asked for the catalyst before you got here on earth to help you change or produce something that will affect many people in a positive way. This means that the fire under your behind is blazing on purpose. The best way to determine this is to have someone run your natal astrological chart and a current chart to see what may or may not be attributing factors to your situation.

Just working magick to relieve a crossed condition won't help you any if you don't work through the problem or situation to resolution. The crossed condition will occur repeatedly until you make up your mind to do something about it—and make an effort to solve the problem.

Uncrossing Colors

The magickal community is always diverse in its teachings, so it is no surprise that as we look through various written materials, we find several color combinations used to relieve a crossed condition. Some magickal people prefer to use the double-action candles, where others like to choose individual tapers or votives. With individual candles, some may pick purples and blues, where others opt for the trinity of yellow, orange, and brown. In the latter example, the orange and yellow are to promote positive vibrations and speed things ahead, where the brown is used to banish any negative energies that may be hanging around. Purple and blue seek the higher octaves of energy. It is helpful to burn a white candle after you have completed magickal work, along with saying an affirmation aloud that matches your future intent.

Reversals

Many of the spells in the following chapters come under the heading of "reversals," meaning that we are returning energy sent to us rather than feeding a problem with our own negative energy. Whether or not you want to use the person's name who is doing rotten things to you in the spell is entirely up to you. Some magickal practitioners feel that you shouldn't target anyone at all (simply indiscriminately send it back and it will be fine), others think that it is perfectly acceptable to give the junk right back to the person who started it thank-you-very-much, and others think that hey, an eye for an eye and all that. This all falls back to "my way is the right way" mode of thought, something I personally try to stay away from. Me? I'm a moon in Sagittarius, straddle-the-fence kind of gal, meaning, "You're on your own here, honey."

Curses

If you think you are cursed—stop! Real curses—true curses—
are incredibly rare. Most people don't have the magickal
expertise or time to whale you with a good one, and if they
do have that kind of power at their fingertips, they are most
likely well trained, which means, basically, you're not worth
the trouble (unless, of course, you've done something incredibly criminal and then you darned well deserve it). All kidding
aside, many people who think they are cursed are really suf-
fering from low self-esteem or some sort of mental incapacity,
and therefore, the curse is all in their head.

Of course, it may seem very real to them, but that is
because they are feeding their own monster of creation. I've
found that putting this type of individual in touch with his
or her guardian angel to be very effective. Assisting them in
developing their own spiritual plan that concentrates on positive affirmations, simple light-geared rituals, meditation, and
prayer will also help to alleviate the situation. Unfortunately,
I'll warn you now, many times it is easier to think you are
cursed than to go through all the hard work of a spiritual

plan, and many times those in need will snub their noses at your suggestions. If this happens, they are in denial. (Which, the last time I checked, was a psychological condition, not the result of a spell.) The best mode of thought here is to send the individual to someone who could truly help them (like a psychotherapist or other medical doctor) and offer to pray for them in the meantime.

Finally, watch out for the yo-yos who tell you that a curse hangs over your head. Sometimes people do this just for spite, other times it is for money. If someone lies about a curse, then, in reality, they are actually cursing themselves. The Karma goes back to them and you can just whistle a merry tune and move forward with your life. If the statement really starts to bother you, do a cleansing ritual and forget it.

Stay Frosty Spell

Sometimes when negative things occur we wish the events would just stop spinning long enough to catch our breath and think things through. We also want to use this time to take control. Anger is not an option. This little spell helps you do just that.

The rosary was an instrument of worship of the rose, which ancient Rome knew as the Flower of Venus and the badge of her sacred prostitutes.[2] Where the red rose represented sexuality, the white rose (or lily) represented purity. The Christians adopted both symbolic flowers and changed their meanings to fit the new faith. Some scholars feel that the rose was first used in India, where the Great Mother was addressed as the Holy Rose. It is no wonder, then, that the magickal symbolism of the rose involves passion, pure love, friendship, and sexuality. The combination of

---

2. Barbara Walker, *The Woman's Encyclopedia of Myths and Secrets* (New York: Harper Collins, 1983), p. 866.

honey, rose, and spring water in this spell draws the purity of mind in perfect love and perfect trust, allowing you to relax, see clearly, and buy some time to think about your circumstances.

Supplies: The event in question, written on a small piece of paper; 2 small cups (or shot glasses); 3 pinches sea salt; spring water; a lock of your hair; 3 drops honey; a rose petal.

Instructions: Fold the paper three times. Place in the bottom of the first shot glass. Sprinkle with sea salt. Pour water over top. Put the lock of your hair in the second shot glass. Put three drops of honey on the hair. Add the rose petal. Cover with spring water. Say:

Time stops, hatred drops
into the vast, frozen pool of the underworld.
Wisdom comes, fear runs
I have time to make informed decisions.
Time stops, hatred drops
into the vast, frozen pool of the underworld.

> Gentle breezes, power freezes
> I have time to see every reason.
> Time stops, hatred drops
> into the vast, frozen pool of the underworld.
> So mote it be.

Draw an equal-armed cross (page 65) over both glasses to seal the spell. Freeze both glasses. Thaw the glasses when you are ready to deal logically with the situation.

To enhance this spell:

- Saturn, the planet of constriction, can assist you in slowing things down a bit so you can find that necessary breathing space. Saturn's day is Saturday.

- Employ a rosary in your spell, saying an affirmation when you touch each bead.

Practical Tip

The moon travels on an elliptical path around the earth. The point farthest from the earth is called apogee. The point when the moon is closest to the earth is called perigee. When perigee coincides with the full moon, the moon's ability to reflect energy is magnified. Odd weather conditions, freak storms, strange emotions, and a greater providence for violence and criminal behavior occur. Magickal people learn to harness this power to enhance their workings and obtain their desires.

Melting Misery: Snow Magick

For those of you who live in the winter climes, you might like
to try working with snow. First, draw a large pentacle in the
snow. Stand in the center of the pentacle and repeat the
chant on pages 122–123 or use another of your choosing.
Gauge your spell to the weather conditions. For example, if
you live in an area where you receive lots of snow (and fast
melting is not an option), repeat the above spell as given. For
those of you who live further south, where snow storms are
intermittent and melting will occur in a few days or a week,
change your spell to give you a specific amount of time (one
day, three days, seven days, etc.). Each day, as the pentacle
melts, stand in the center and repeat your purpose, ending
with a positive affirmation. Walk along the lines of the star so
as not to ruin your snow pentacle. For those of you who live
in areas where ice storms are prevalent, but have little snow,
fashion your pentacle with rock salt on the sheets of ice
(you'll have to do this one on a sidewalk or other concrete
surface as the rock salt will kill the sleeping grass). In areas
where there is no chance of snow, you can make a smaller

version of the snow pentacle on a plate with crushed ice; place your name in the center, as well as your desire, then place in the freezer. Allow to thaw when you're ready to deal.

To perform an ice and fire spell, make your plate pentacle with snow or crushed ice and place one birthday candle at each point. Seal this spell with an ice cube set against a lower point of the pentacle; freeze. When you are ready to cast your spell, put the plate on the altar and light the candles, saying the appropriate incantation. This is very nice for a full moon perigee ceremony where you need lots of power. (If you need to break the spell quickly, run hot water over the frozen pentacle.)

Bringing Pressure to Bear

Scholars have connected mistletoe with early Pagan rites, symbolizing fertility and the issue of the sacrificed God. Another folk belief adopted by the Christian Church, mistletoe was carried to the High Altar on Christmas Eve, though some church officials later denied the import or significance, saying the mistletoe was placed there in error. Magickally, mistletoe carries the power of protection, fertility, health, love, exorcism, and hunting. In this spell we're going to rely on its exorcism and protection qualities. If you want something to move, then here is what you do.

Supplies: A big, fat, heavy book; holy water; sage; the issue written on a piece of paper and the conclusion you desire (be specific); crushed mistletoe; a 13-inch piece of red yarn; 1 red candle. (**Note:** For clarity on a love issue, use rose petals instead of mistletoe.)

Instructions: Sprinkle the book with holy water. Cleanse the work area and the book with burning sage. Open the book. Place the paper in the center of the open book. Sprinkle the mistletoe over your paper. Lay the red yarn across the page so that part of the yarn is on the page and part of the yarn will be hanging out of the book when it is closed. This yarn is your "release" should circumstances not manifest as you desired. If this happens, you can pull the yarn out of the book to break the spell. Hold your hands over the open book, and say:

Up through my roots, down through my wings,
into my core, energy sings.
Through mind gone still, through words that dance,
descend upon me, sacred trance.
Let all impediments to grace
now be banished from this place.
Salted water, smoke of sage,
cast out all trace of fear and rage.

Close the book. Place the red candle on top of the book.
Relax, take a deep breath, and visualize harmony around
you. Light the candle. Hold your fingertips on the book.
Increase the pressure with your fingers as you recite:

Spirits of east, south, west, north,
I summon, stir, and call ye forth.
Graces of thought, change, feeling, fact—
these gifts now let your strength attract.

O Lady, Queen of Earth and Sea
come to my aid, I cry to thee.
O Lord of Air, O Lord of Fire,
come and bring form to my desire.

O light that rises, light that spins,
I raise you as the Work begins.
O swirling cone of power, I pray
that you do just as I say.

Pressure to bear, enchantment begins
Explode the energy so I will win.
The spirits speak, the serpent curls
The dead assist and change unfurls.

O Mighty Ones, you are released
with thanks and love by this your priest
O Circle, open your embrace.
O Power, to your task make haste.

Sun, Moon, Stars, Planets, now hear ye—
align yourselves compatibly!
Let no reversal trouble me—
as is my will, so mote it be![3]

Clap your hands to seal the spell. When you have
received your desire, burn the paper and scatter the
herbs in the wind.

----

3. All-purpose chant written by Jack Veasey.

To enhance this spell:

- Perform on Tuesday in the hour of Mars.

- Perform on a full moon.

- Add the symbol of Jupiter (expansive), Mercury (clear communication), or Mars (action) to the candle.

- Add a pinch of ginger to the mix to make the spell work faster.

Four Thieves Vinegar Recipe

The progeny of Bayou country, you'll find recipes for Four Thieves Vinegar in many of the occult texts produced between 1940 and the late 1960s. In the 1970s, when the New Age craze hit the eastern seaboard, this little concoction began to slowly fade from predominant books on Witchcraft, but solidly remained in use in the Big Easy (New Orleans) and surrounding areas. A powerful little formula, this recipe turns back evil and negativity, right to the lap where it belongs. Use to dress or load in candles, add a drop or two while mixing your incenses, or dress objects used as a focal point for returning negativity. This particular recipe comes from Morgana, of Morgana's Chamber in New York City. I would like to add here that some Four Thieves Vinegar recipes can be consumed. Those recipes include turned red wine (red wine that has turned to vinegar) or wine vinegar and garlic. **Note:** This one is not to be ingested!

Supplies: An 8-ounce glass jar (empty and sterilized); 6 ounces red wine vinegar; 11 drops vetivert oil; 9 drops High John the Conqueror oil; 5 pinches ground black pepper; 3 pinches crushed vervain; 3 pinches sea salt.

Instructions: Add ingredients in order given, concentrating on protection from enemies, both magickal and mundane. Cap tightly and store. Best made on the dark moon.

Uses:

- Soak cotton balls in Four Thieves Vinegar to keep ghosts and evil influences away.

- Dress a black or brown candle in Four Thieves Vinegar for protection and exorcism.

- Sprinkle Four Thieves Vinegar on the porch or stoop of an individual who has been harassing you to overcome their evil intentions.

- Fill a small bottle with Four Thieves Vinegar. Write down the person's name that you wish to be banished from your life. Throw into a living body of water.

Mirror Work to Repel Negativity

If you know that there is negativity galloping toward you (and yes, sometimes the Fates are kind enough to warn us), you can set up a "trap-matrix" with a fluorite crystal and a small mirror. The crystal is charged to direct harmful energy to a small mirror, wherein the universe takes that energy and sends it to where Spirit thinks best. The only warning attached to this spell rests on your concentration and ability to focus. Your concentration requires that you see the mirror as a funnel, wherein energy can move in only one direction: toward the surface of the mirror, making the mirror a small, open doorway through which energy can pass in only one direction, through the mirror and away from you.

You can also use this mirror work to trap one of those things-that-go-bump-in-the-night-and-you-have-tried-every-thing-and-it-won't-go-away scenarios. To do this, set the mirror up as a bind where the doorway is like spirit-sticky-paper, then bury the mirror in a location off your property where it is most likely not to be disturbed.[4] Remember, you should do a thorough house cleansing first. If that doesn't work, use the mirror, then do an additional cleansing of the home.

Mirrors and other reflective surfaces were once regarded as soul-catchers and doorways to the spirit world. The Egyptian word for "life" was synonymous with the word for "mirror." Magickal practitioners have long used mirrors to gain second sight, believing that if a mirror could accurately reflect the physical, it would accurately reflect both the past and the future if tuned in a specific way.

----

4. Lady Gillian.

To Stop a Particularly Bad Case of Gossip

People gossip because they are not happy with their own lives, and therefore feel the overriding need to share their misery by making other people unhappy. If you've tried the minor folk magick above and they haven't worked, here's something that was designed for my daughter when she had a particularly difficult time at school with a clique of girls who were set on destroying her reputation.

Supplies: 4 black candles; protection oil (see page 40); your picture; salt; the names of the people who are spreading rumors about you (if you don't have their names, then say, "All detrimental talk about me ceases immediately," and write this on a piece of paper); 1 red candle.

Instructions: Dress the black candles with the protection oil, working from the bottom of the candle up to the taper. Set the candles around your picture. Draw a circle of salt around the four candles so that the circle encloses

the candles and your picture. Light the candles. Say the
following:

> **O Mighty Mother. There are people**
> **who imagine things about me that are not true.**
> **Those who consider themselves the Kings and**
> **Queens of** *(school, my job, our family, etc.)*
> **have set themselves against me.**
> **They have enticed those in authority to harm me.**
> **Be my shield, great Mother.**
> **Arise and cover me with the glory of your essence.**

Place the names of the people who are trying to destroy
you under the red candle. Light this candle. Hold both
of your hands over the candle (not too close) and say:

> **Break their hold upon me asunder,**
> **and cast away the physical and astral lines**
> **of negative energy attached to me.**
> **Provide me with the tools**
> **to fight for my reputation.**

Look down upon them, my Mother.
Let them feel your wrath as you
return their negative energies to them
and break them to pieces like a potter's vessel.
In the names of the Lord and Lady, make it so!

Clap your hands and proclaim loudly:

This spell is sealed!

Allow the candles to burn completely. It is okay to perform this spell every day until you feel that you are no longer subject to harm.

To enhance this spell:

• Perform on Friday in the hour of Venus or the hour of Mercury.

• Inscribe the symbols of Venus and Mercury on your candles.

• Add a compelling oil when dressing the candles.

- Prepare a Return to Sender Powder and sprinkle where you know the gossip will walk. Ingredients: Yellow talc; rose (protection); frankincense (protection); vetivert (curse-breaking); honeysuckle (protection); angelica (curse-breaking); thistle (curse-breaking).

- Burn the names and scatter the ashes to the wind. Say, "I was bound, now I am free."

Condescending Bending

There is nothing more irritating than when someone treats you in a condescending manner because of your age, gender, religious choice, education, race, etc. Try this spell to gain equal footing.

Supplies: 4 white candles; 1 onion; 1 black marker; a mortar and pestle; a pinch of basil; ¼ teaspoon brown sugar.

Instructions: On the full moon, light the four white candles, asking for the assistance of Spirit and your ancestors. Peel the onion all the way to the core. Visualize the discrimination against you peeling away.

Save the onion skins. Under the full moon, bury the onion pieces, but not the skins. Write the individual's name on the onion skins with the black marker. With the mortar and pestle, crush the onion skins, basil, and brown sugar until you have a very fine mix. Hold your hands over the mixture, and say:

> **You think you're smart**
> **You think you're hot**
> **But this magick powder**
> **Will make you stop!**

Sprinkle your magick powder where you are sure they will walk. If you have a particularly nasty case of discrimination, add red pepper to the mix.[5]

---

5. For additional information on magickal powders, see my book *To Light a Sacred Flame* (St. Paul, MN: Llewellyn, 1999).

Nasties on the Internet

Although I find the Internet useful for research, advertise-
ment, and general communication, I have discovered that the
net brings out the worst in some people, especially those with
low self-esteem. The anonymity of the net and its freedom
for solitary use makes some people think that just because
you can't see them, or reach through their monitor and pinch
them, they can say just about anything to you. I've also discovered that not everyone who can type can write. Many
times statements that the Internet user may think innocuous
upon typing blare something across the net that the writer
didn't mean at all. Many a list serve has been pulled due to a
simple, misunderstood statement that flares into a horrid
argument. There are also the sneaky cut-'n-pasters (I've been
a victim of this more than once) who copy your e-mail, add
or take out what they wish, then forward the information on
to many people, as if this was what you originally wrote.
Because we humans are in the habit of taking things at face
value, we forget that people do pull such shenanigans.

The first rule of thumb when an argument occurs is to simply disengage. Who are they anyway, but words on a screen? I know it gets under your skin, but in a few days (hopefully) you'll forget all about it. If the missive has really bothered you to the point where you can't sleep (Goddess forbid), then try the following spell.

Supplies: A copy of the e-mail, conversation, or website.

Instructions: Fold the paper into a boat shape. Hey, get creative! If you can go to a pond or stream (or the ocean), that would be great. If not, then fill your sink or bathtub. Cast your little boat adrift, saying:

> **Tempest toss and Neptune's wrath**
> **I give the negative energy back.**
> **Adrift upon the sea words**
> **you sink from Neptune's deadly scourge.**
> **From cyberspace to Davey's Locker**
> **Your words become a shadow stalker.**
> **They slip and slide around you now**
> **Upon your deck, across your bow.**
> **From port to starboard they tighten the grip**
> **Alas, alack . . . you sunk your ship!**

Sink the boat. Expect them to be off-line for awhile. Of course, this only works if you did not start the argument.

Nightmares

We all have nightmares now and then, but if they plague you it can be extremely frustrating. When your sleep is disturbed by frightening images on a regular basis, you should seek professional counseling as this means you are consciously suppressing an issue or event in your past (or present) and your subconscious has had enough of your denial. For the occasional nightmare, place the following blessed sleep mixture in a white, green, blue, or purple square of cloth. Tie, place under your pillow, and enjoy pleasant dreams.

Blessed Sleep Mixture

Supplies: Mix equal parts of lavender (blessed sleep), vervain (enchantment), allspice (improves concentration and study habits), pine (peace of mind and strength), orange peel (cleansing), and chamomile (easy sleep).

Other ideas for a restful sleep:

• Place crushed garlic under the bed to frighten away bad dreams.

• Empower a stuffed animal for a child that acts as a guard against nightmares.

• Hang an empowered dream catcher or hex sign over your bed.

• Sew a quilt for a child using protective needle and thread magick. Make pockets that can hold herbs and be sewn shut.

• Add a sprinkle of angelica to all wash water for nightclothes and sheets to exorcise any negativity. This is especially good for the sick.

• Place an amethyst on the night table. Amethyst is well known for soaking up negativity.

• Mix ground coffee and cinnamon with a mortar and pestle. Burn on a charcoal brick to fumigate the room.

Medical Madness

Ever have a month or string of events where you are constantly going to the doctor or ferrying family members back and forth to various medical establishments? When the checking account dips precariously low and you view each day with frantic disbelief, you might want to try this spell.

Supplies: Pictures of your family who have been affected (and those who aren't); a plastic baggie large enough to hold the pictures; thyme (good health); black pepper; 2 small hand mirrors that you can purchase at a craft or drug store.

Instructions: Put the pictures in the bag. Sprinkle with thyme, asking Spirit to send blessings and good health to your family. Set the baggie on your altar or on a place that will not be disturbed. Surround with a circle of black pepper (to make enemies—in this case, sickness—flee). Put one mirror facing the street, outside, by your front door. Do the same for the back door. Visualize all evil turning back before entering your home.

Fanatic Flytrap

Deceptively simple. Frighteningly powerful. This little spell works wonders to catch (and hold) someone who is trying to harm you.

Single and double spirals figure prominently in Neolithic Europe. Spiral oculi—double twists that resemble a pair of eyes—are found in places like Newgrange in Ireland, connected with the philosophy of death and rebirth (the sacred cycle from all which life is bound). The counterclockwise spiral, which this spell uses, appeared in the Euphrates cultures as early as 2000 B.C. In Egypt, it meant "the country that one returns to," meaning that by using the counterclockwise spiral in magick, you are sending something back to where it came from. Both clockwise and counterclockwise spirals represent movement.

Supplies: A piece of paper that fits over the mouth of the jar with room to spare; 1 small glass Mason jar; a black marker; 7 nails; ½ ounce gel glue; a sturdy rubber band (or the ring top of the Mason jar).

Instructions: Place the paper over the mouth of the jar. Bend down the corners to make the circular impression of the mouth of the jar on the paper. Use this impression to draw a sacred spiral that begins from the outside and curls to the very center of the circle. Allow to dry. On a small slip of paper, write the fanatic's name. If you do not know the name, write, "The person who is sending me negative mail (or whatever)." Put the nails and the paper in the jar. Shake three times. Remove the paper and drizzle glue over the nails. Cover the jar with the paper, aligning your sacred spiral so that it is directly over the mouth of the jar. Cap with the ring or a strong rubber band. Tap the jar seven times. Then say:

Ever winding, ever coiling
Trapped into the center.
Ever moving, ever circling
Pulled into the center.
Ever prancing, ever dancing
Drawn toward the center.
You can't hurt me
You can't see me
Stuck inside this jar!

Trace the spiral, from the outside in, with your finger, visualizing the individual who is bothering you being caught and dragged into the jar. When you have finished, tap the sides of the jar nine times, repeating the individual's name or a description of the negativity with each tap. As the glue hardens, their negativity will cling to them like glue, keeping them too busy to bother with you!

Stolen Limelight

Okay, we can't all be at the top of the heap at the same time, and you will lose out to other people many times in your life. You just have to learn to live with it—that's part of learning how to mature, grow strong, and keep working toward capturing your dreams. It's when you fail due to the unscrupulous, underhanded actions of others, however, that it hurts the most. Fair is fair! This spell is to give you back the limelight you so richly deserve by using the energy of the planet Uranus, the Great Changer. **Caution:** If you have been deceitful or immoral in your own dealings, this spell will bring your own actions back on you, too!

Supplies: A black magick marker; 1 new light bulb; 1 burned-out light bulb; 1 small, brown paper bag.

Instructions: There are two parts to this spell. First, write your name in black marker on the new light bulb. Under your name write the word "success." Screw the light bulb into any handy socket. Hold your hands over the bulb, and say:

Energy feeds my success
My work will be the very best!

Relax. Close your eyes and repeat the chant several times
until you slip into a light, altered state. When finished,
open your eyes, take a deep breath, and clap your hands.
Leave the light on until you see evidence of your success,
then, use the light as you normally would.

Now, write the individual(s) name(s) who stole your
thunder on the burned-out light bulb. On the brown
paper bag, draw the symbol for Uranus (♅) twenty-one
times, visualizing the individual being caught up in his
or her own deception.

Say:

Your own deception you will meet
the moment I smash this on the street!

Take the bag outside (wear heavy shoes). Drop it in the
middle of the street. Stomp on it. Bury the bag off your
property.

To enhance this spell:

- Dust your pulse points with cinnamon to ward off jealousy.

- Continue to work on positive PR for yourself (not bragging—honest stuff, please).

- Carry a personal charm bag that includes cinquefoil, cinnamon, and angelica. These herbs encourage truth, prosperity, and protection.

Midnight Callers

With today's modern equipment you can easily put call-block on your phone, but what if you've got a tricky person who bips from phone booth to phone booth to harass you, or is smart enough to block his or her own number so you can't figure out the phone number that's generating these ridiculous electronic missives? **Note:** If you are being harassed or stalked by threatening phone calls, keep accurate records, tape the calls if you can, and notify the police and the phone company.

> **Supplies:** Red, white, and black cord, shoestrings, or ribbon; vinegar.

> **Instructions:** Braid the cord. Dip ends in vinegar. Allow to dry. Tie around the receiver cord (if you have a cordless phone, use longer ribbon and tie around the base of the phone). Say:

By the count of one, this spell's begun
(tie a knot on the dangling end of your braid).
By the count of two, *(person's name)* can't get
through. *(Tie a knot above the first.*
If you don't know the person's name, just say,
"the person who is bothering me.")
By count of three, I am free.
(Tie a knot above the last.)
By count of four, you can't bother me any more!
(Tie a knot above the last.)
By count of five, this spell's alive.
(Tie a knot above the last.)
By count of six, the spell is fixed.
(Tie a knot above the last.)
By count of seven, my word is given.
(Tie a knot above the last.)
By count of eight, I seal your fate!
(Tie a knot above the last.)
By count of nine, your mouth I bind!
(Tie a knot above the last.)

Liar, Liar, Pants on Fire

There is nothing more humiliating then having your luck turn on the pivotal action of a liar. One thing that does stop liars and the rumors thereof is the practice of always trying to tell the truth yourself. Sometimes this isn't so easy. For little rumors, the mere act of disengaging from the situation can help you more than if you come out with mouth blazing and fire spewing from your eyeballs; however, there are times when a situation just seems to get worsen, no matter how honest you have been or how calculating your moves. When this happens, try this spell.

Supplies: If you can, get the underwear of the offending party (if this is not possible, buy a pair and write the name of the offending individual in the crotch with black marker); a bottle of the hottest Tabasco sauce you can find; a bit of thistle and nettles; cinquefoil (to urge them to tell the truth); black pepper; rubbing alcohol; a long match; an old cauldron or outside grill.

Instructions: Pour the Tabasco sauce on the crotch of the underwear. Let dry. Sprinkle with herbs and black pepper. Sprinkle with a bit of alcohol (not much). Use a long match to light. Burn in an old cauldron or outside grill. As the underwear burns, say:

> *(The person's name),* I've had enough.
> I rise above you, I've gotten tough.
> The wagging tongues of flame bite back
> I refuse to take your hateful flack!
> Your lies become a conflagration
> Bringing you to degradation.
> Your deceit recedes its clinging grasp
> And I am free—the truth at last!

Scatter the ashes off your property.

Necessary Separation:
The Black Ribbon Spell

A friend of mine once told me that people are like waves of the sea. Sometimes they flow in on time, smoothly, gently, bringing harmony, leaving behind only the gift of Spirit and pristine sand. Other times they come crashing into your life, smashing and destroying. When they leave, you're stuck with all sorts of smelly stuff clinging to the little beach you call your life. There's nothing worse than having to clean up after other people! When a friend, family member, or co-worker takes off leaving bad vibes behind (or won't take off quickly), then the black ribbon spell is what you want to do!

Supplies: 2 white candles; a black ribbon;
   a pair of scissors.

Instructions: Light the white candles. Name one as yourself, and one as the person who is causing you problems (or has left behind unfortunate energies). Tie the black ribbon to both candles, then draw them out as far as the candles will go. Entreat Brigid (Celtic goddess of healing waters and fire) to bring healing to both parties and purge the negativity from your body, mind, and spirit. Ask that the individual be separated from you, that all emotional and energy ties be broken, and that this happen immediately. Calmly, solemnly, cut the ribbon. Allow the candles to burn completely. Throw any remaining wax and the ribbons away. You can use this procedure for an abusive family member, co-worker, or other group environment, too!

In Your Face with Dead Disgrace

From the hills of West Virginia to the bayou of Louisiana, the inclusion of graveyard dirt in numerous spells to cast off negativity and give someone their just desserts has always ridden high on the ingredient list of "favorites that work." This spell is to turn back negativity created by a group (or a select few) who wish to destroy you or your reputation. First, you will need the name of a beloved ancestor or someone who has passed away that cared about you very much. Then, once you have made this choice, you can get on with your spell. I warn you, this spell is a little more complicated than the others.

Supplies: 1 cauldron filled with fresh sand; a lime for each person in the plot; a black marker; vinegar; the following ingredients ground together into a fine powder: garden nightshade, garlic, old, dried coffee grounds, red pepper, black pepper, and nettles; a black candle dipped in honey and rolled in cobwebs and graveyard dirt.

Instructions: Cast a circle of protection. Draw a pentacle in the sand inside the cauldron with your finger. Write the name of each person in the plot on a lime. (Stick an extra lime in there for those who are helping, but you don't know who they are.) Cut a hole in the top of each lime, careful not to smear the names. Put one drop of vinegar in each lime. Fill the hole in the lime with your herbal mix. Place the limes in the cauldron in a circle or at the points of the pentacle.

Turn out the lights. Take a deep breath. Seat yourself before the cauldron. Light the black candle, and say:

> **Dark Mother, Goddess of Justice,**
> **Come to me. Be with me.**
> **Hear me. Help me.**

Take a deep breath and visualize the Dark Goddess coming toward you, holding out her hands to help you. Think of an ancestor you trust to help you, and say:

> **Ancestor,** *(say the name),*
> **I am in need of assistance.**
> **Come to me. Be with me.**
> **Hear me. Help me.**

Take a deep breath and visualize who you have called coming to your aid. Hold your hands over each lime in turn, and say:

Remove their power.
Wrap them in the web of their own deceit.
Bury them in their own lies.
May your support desert you.
Failure closes around you.
May your plot be revealed,
And justice be your meal.
May your courage leave you.
May your words trip you.
Your unfair desires will come to nothing.
May you be downed by your own stupidity.
So mote it be!

Allow the candle to burn completely. Throw the limes on their property, where they work, or where they go to school.

Reminder: You must get rid of the limes. If they remain in your home or apartment, the limes will act like a magnet for their evil intentions. If there is no possible way that you can put the limes near the individual in question, throw the limes in the middle of a crossroads in the dead of night—you must get them away from you.

Note: If you don't want to use real graveyard dirt, you can mix the following substitute: Equal parts of mullein, wormwood, patchouli, alder, mandrake, and black talc (or black glitter).

Big Mama Mush 'Em Spell

Throughout my career as a mother of four children, I have had a few instances where adults (for whatever reason) have deemed it necessary to target one of my children. When this happens I check my bank account, then head to the candle store. I buy as many black candles as I can afford, and one purple candle. On the purple candle, inscribe the astrological sign of Saturn ($\hbar$).

Supplies: As many black candles as you can afford; 1 purple candle.

Instructions: I begin the spell by laying out a large pentacle on the table and putting a black candle at each point. Then, with as many candles as I have, I begin to fill in the lines of the pentacle.

As I arrange the candles, I think about turning back the negativity. I think of all that horrid dark energy (that I didn't create) nesting securely in the arms of the individual(s) who created the energy in the first place. Then, I ask my ancestors to be with me and help me in my hour

of need, and light a purple candle as an offering to them.
Use this simple chant to draw the dead to you:

Come be one
Become
Be one!

Keep chanting until you reach a light, altered state.
Imagine the dead drawing around you in a circle of
powerful, white energy as you chant. When you feel
they are present, take a deep breath, open your eyes,
state your purpose, and light the black candles. Thank
the dead for helping you. Let the black candles (and the
purple one) burn completely.

To enhance this spell:

- Perform on a full moon.

- Perform on the dark of the moon.

- Perform on a Saturday.

- Perform during an eclipse of the moon (check what sign
  the moon is in for further information on how your spell
  will react).

Stirring Up Chaos

Now and then a bit of chaos is what you need to provide a smokescreen until you can get some time to think, or to protect your interests until the right person can make a good decision for you (such as in a job promotion). The goddess chosen for this one (a favorite of mine, and useful for oh-so-many difficulties) is Sekhmet, the Egyptian goddess of magick, war, justice, demi-animals, courage, wild animals, fire, hunting, and physical strength. Her nickname, The Powerful, and her reputation as a pitiless opponent make her an excellent choice for this spell.

Supplies: Your stove (or backyard grill); a pot or cauldron; spring water; a wooden spoon; a yellow or gold candle.

Instructions: Fill the pot with spring water and set on a heated surface. Bring to a boil. Stir slowly, counterclockwise (widdershins), with the wooden spoon. Think about the situation. As the water begins to boil and the steam rises, envision the steam as a protective vapor that surrounds you. As you stir, ask Spirit to add the right amount of chaos to the mix to keep you from being harmed. Finally, draw in Sekhmet, in all her glory, asking her to protect you and boil your enemies in their own evil intentions. As an offering, burn a gold or yellow candle in her honor. Call her with the following chant:

> Goddess of the fire and mother of strength,
> Sekhmet, come to me, come to me.
> Goddess of justice, mother of power,
> Sekhmet, be with me, be with me.
> Goddess of battle, victory mother,
> Sekhmet, stay with me, stay with me.
> Heart pounding, jungle stomping,
> Sekhmet, bring them chaos!

Warning: This spell *will* create chaos, so don't let yourself get swept up in the panic and think nothing is happening to help you. Be patient. It may take from five to seven days for you to actually see results in your favor, this is assuming that in the meantime, you have done the work required and performed additional magick.

4

When Things Get Sticky

*T*he spells and rituals in this chapter are designed for some of those complicated or more unfortunate matters; however, a spell should not be used in place of professional medical care or necessary intervention by the proper authorities.

Hang 'Em High

Ever had one of those months (or years) when it seems that
those big corporations have targeted you? Of course, we
know that those policies were made by a person (or small
group of people) and that a single person (or a smaller group
of people) carries them out. Usually, you can get the name of
at least one of these people (but you have to be careful, as
someone may be carrying out their job with no personal mal-
ice to you). Then, there are those instances where the person
you are dealing with is the root of your difficulties (you know
this for a fact) and they are using the power of the business to
make you miserable.

   The use of poppet or doll magick is so old that it gives the
scholarly mind lots of room for argument and interpretation.
We do know that these dolls were never meant to provide
hours of play in the enchanted realm of a child's make-
believe. Poppets are designed to represent real people, or in
this case, a person attached to the living entity of a company.
In order for the poppet to work, you must have something
that is in sympathy with the individual or, in this case, the

corporation. Poppets can be used effectively in healing spells or in spells like this one where the intent is not to harm, but to balance the energies of the universe in a petition of fair treatment.

Supplies: Straight pins; red vinegar; crushed garlic; enough strips of paper to list the names of those trying to cheat you and the situation; 1 doll (sex appropriate); a 13-inch black cord; the company logo or name (letterhead or business card is good); black thread.

Instructions: Dip the pins in the red vinegar. Let dry. Roll in crushed garlic. Pin the names of all the people who you know are involved in your problem on the clothing of the doll. Write "unknown" on one piece of paper to encompass anyone who is involved that you are unaware of. Tie the cord onto the right ankle of the doll. Hang upside down, as if the doll has been caught in a trap. Sew the business card or other representation of the name to the feet of the doll with black thread. Say:

**Deception uncovered, you are discovered,
balance is restored, I won't be ignored!**

Repeat the chant until you move into an altered state, then clap your hands to seal the spell. When the truth comes out, and you are totally repaid, burn the papers, throw the pins in a crossroads, and release the doll into the garbage bin.

To enhance this spell:

• Remember to keep accurate records. This is just as important as the magick.

• Sprinkle the clothing of the doll with justice incense.

• Perform on Tuesday, or in the hour of Mars, or at the full moon.

To Bring an Animal Killer or Abuser to Justice

To work with the following goddess, a little research is required, thus we turn to Willow. With her incisive prose, we learning the following:

The Morrigan, or Morrig to the Ancient Irish, is a challenging and paradoxical figure, shifting from unearthly beauty to hideousness, from helpfulness to hindrance. There is some disagreement among scholars as to the correct translation of her name: Great Queen or Phantom Queen. From experience, both names apply.

In legend she is often associated with battle, hence her designation of Battle Queen. Looking beneath the visceral aspects of war, these early conflicts were often a matter of sovereignty and self-determination. As Great Queen, Goddess of the Land, she guards and sustains her chosen people.

In an age when most of us do not bear the responsibility of the welfare of our tribe, its territory and herds of cattle, sovereignty takes on a more personal meaning. The vocation of sovereign requires awareness, self-control, and a strong sense of personal responsibility. These same traits apply to sovereignty on an individual level.

Personal sovereignty necessitates a strong center and an awareness of our strengths and weaknesses, not for ego inflation or neurotic obsession but in the wisdom of self-knowledge. Self-knowledge is a tricky thing; from birth we are told repeatedly who and what we are. Add to this the inevitable baggage we gather along the way and the question "Who am I?" takes on stunning complexity. Fortunately much of our self and the reasons for our behavior lie within our unconscious mind. Enter the realm of the Phantom Queen. As the Old Woman of Knowledge, the Morrig champions our search for wholeness, challenging our conceptions of our selves and our environment. As we bring to light the artifacts of our lives, as we disengage the patterns of our most onerous behaviors, the Morrig stands beside the Well of Life, handing us, if we dare take it, the Cup of Truth, the Truth of Ourselves.[1]

-----

1. Willow Ragan is a writer and visual artist with a degree in photography. Her Craft studies began in 1978 and have included various traditions. Currently living in the wilds of the Ohio Valley, she is the editor of *Leaves*, a publication of the Temple of Danaan.

Once upon a time in the town of we-can't-say-the-name, there was a big pet store with a flashy sign and lots of neat stuff to buy for your pet. They also sold, of course, animals to the consumer who sought the love of adorable cuddly things. Everyone thought the new store was just a wonderful idea, and many of us frequented the place to pick up neat and nifty things for our pets. At the same time, a very attractive young woman joined the Black Forest Family (my tradition). At the night of her dedication she told us that this wonderful pet store was not so wonderful a place. Any animal they could not sell in a specific amount of time, they sold to scientific organizations for experimentation purposes. In fact, they were making more money on this type of sale than on their entire store merchandise combined, and so they purposefully overstocked on their animals (especially the fluffy, furry kind). The store, she had discovered, was only a front. Was there anything that my students could do?

We can thank David Norris for the words, and a very enterprising and brave lady for her actions.

Dark Goddess Powder

Supplies: Black talc; dried nightshade; dried nettles; black cat hair or dog hair.

Instructions: As you are making the powder, repeat the incantation below to the Raven Mother (The Morrigan):

At this hour of our protection
I call thee, Raven Mother, COME!
Sweep your broom of intercession
I call thee, Raven Mother, COME!
Your wings descend in instant fury
I call thee, Raven Mother, COME!
Shatter doubt, dread fear and worry
I call thee, Raven Mother, COME!
Send your lightening, fire and thunder
I call thee, Raven Mother, COME!
Let these wrongs be ripped asunder
I call thee, Raven Mother, COME!
May no voice be raised against you
I call thee, Raven Mother, COME!

Shout down the lies and see us through
I call thee, Raven Mother, COME!
Let no hand be turned against us
I call thee, Raven Mother, COME!
Let your winds of truth be endless
I call thee, Raven Mother, COME!
Seal your spell so all may hear it
I call thee, Raven Mother, COME!
Loose your hounds of blood and spirit
I call thee, Raven Mother, COME!
And when these ills are all rejected
I call thee, Raven Mother, COME!
I'll dwell within your cloak, protected
I call thee, Raven Mother, COME![2]

Our friend visited the establishment, taking her time going around the store. She sprinkled the powder all around—on shelves, the floor, even on the cash register (how she did that, I'll never know!). Each time she sprinkled the powder, she whispered, "I call thee, Raven

---

2. Copyright ©1998 David Norris.

Mother, COME!" She also put protection oil on as many animal cages as she could. It took three months. Eventually, however, the owner of the store was arrested on drug trafficking charges, his wife left him, and the store was sold to better management.

To enhance this spell:

- Perform on a Saturday afternoon around 3:00 P.M. or on Saturday morning at 1:00 A.M.

- Perform on the dark of the moon.

- If you can, get the hair from the abused animal to add to your spellworking. Ask the spirit of the animal to assist you.

Break Apart Those Who Stand Against You

If a group of people has bonded together to seek your destruction, you need to separate them to remove the energy of the bond.

Supplies: Cinquefoil; mustard; and a list of all the people you know that are working against you.

Instructions: On a large piece of paper, wherever you desire, write the first name like this:

Amy Latchaw/separate

Amy Latchaw/separate

Amy Latchaw/separate

Upside down, on a different area of the paper, write the next name, the same way. If there are only two people, write the person's name upside down under the first. If there are more, keep turning the paper and putting them any old place, though for four, you can put them in the four directions, all upside down to show them moving away from each other. Sprinkle with cinquefoil and mustard to bring confusion. (**Note:** This will only work if they have been untruthful.)

Paper spells are by far the easiest type to employ and can be as effective as an all-out ritual, which makes them deceptive indeed. Many individuals feel that a few slashes of the pen on a simple piece of paper carries no power—this is a misguided assumption.

Hold the paper in your hand, and say:

> **Cease, desist, separate, and break apart**
> **Dissolve, divided, detached, disunited.**
> **I call the earth to bind my spell**
> **Air to speed its travel well**
> **Fire to destroy and pull them apart**
> **Water to sooth my aching heart.**
> **So mote it be!**

Draw an equal-armed cross (page 65) in the air to seal the spell. Keep the paper in a safe place until the dissolution takes place, then burn the paper.

If you want to add extra action to the pot, whip up some confusion powder. Use vetivert (curse-breaking and anti-theft); lavender (protection); angelica (cleansing); black pepper (flee evil); and a burnt, knotted shoelace. Grind to a fine powder. Sprinkle over above spell paper or where you know those who wish to harm you will walk.

To enhance this spell:

- Perform on a Saturday in the hour of Saturn.

- Perform on the dark of the moon or the full moon.

- Perform on Tuesday in the hours of Mars or Saturn.

- Because paper spells take less time than other spell techniques, pay closer attention to the timing. For example, do not perform this spell (or any spell) when the moon is void of course. Also, if Mars or Saturn are retrograde, the work may take longer to manifest; however, a Saturn retrograde would be terrific for this spell, as those energies lend well to shaking up groups and organizations to bring justice. For this type of information you will need to turn to one of the many astrological almanacs on the market. It doesn't cost you much to pick up one of these yearly planners and it will certainly pay for itself many times over in your magickal practice.

- On the flip side of this you can bind them so tightly together that they can't stand each other, resulting in the same occurrence—dissipation of the group.

I Want My Stuff Back!

All righty then—you've been traded in for a new model and left high and dry, without a dime in your pocket. Maybe your roommate moved out and took half your stuff with her. What do you do? If Spirit moves someone out of your life, most likely this was the right thing to happen for you. But that's real hard to take when you are hurting, especially if the person who left you tried to harm you too (like clean out your bank account, take the car that was registered in your name, and run off with your familiar). The idea here is not to harm anyone, but to recover what is rightfully yours.

Most of us have read our horoscopes from time to time, but few of us realize the powerful energies the planets represent, not only in our natal chart, but in the dialogue produced daily as they dance through the heavens. The old adage, as above—so below, lets us know that in astrology, what is in the heavens is reflected on earth, and what is on earth is reflected in the heavens.

In this spell we're going to use two vibrant energies, Mars and Mercury. Mars is the quintessential activator energy in the heavens. This planet kick-starts anything that comes close enough for dialogue, and symbolizes action, assertion, will, focus, courage, passion, the ability to outlast enemies, and, when needed, boosts our survival instinct. Mars always reminds me of a precocious child—you know, the one you look for in a group when amusing tricks come to light.

Mercury is the great communicator, with the added bene-fit of swift, quicksilver movement. This planetary energy represents the principle of intellect and unemotional, rational, objective thought, and is a wonderful energy to use when you are worried that your heart is not being honest with your best interests. This planet also concerns your speech and, coupled with the rune Asa (ᚨ), gives you an extra edge for that public speaking venture or talking yourself out of a difficult situation. Combining these Mars and Mercury planetary energies in a spell gives extra power married to clear, high-velocity energy.

Supplies: Cayenne pepper; nettles; red talc; a red marker; a small brandy snifter or glass bowl; a picture of the individual that took your belongings.

Instructions: Grind the pepper, nettles, and talc together. With the red marker, draw the astrological symbol of Mars (♂) on the snifter with the red marker. Beside it draw the symbol for Mercury (☿). Drop the picture in the snifter then cover with the herbal mixture. Say:

Conscience itch

Conscience scratch

You won't find relief

'Til my stuff comes back.

Keep repeating the spell, then list exactly what was stolen from you or hasn't been paid. If you don't get your things back in thirty days, do the spell again. If it's money you're missing, you might want to burn a bayberry candle, asking for the spirit of prosperity to enter your home, especially over any holiday where your family usually outlays a large amount of cash.

To enhance this spell:

- Perform on Tuesday in the hour of Mercury.

- Perform on Wednesday in the hour of Mars.

- Add a red candle (for action) inscribed with the symbols of Mercury and Mars.

- Use the god Mercury as your archetype.

Your Cold, Black Heart

Sometimes there are just people in this world who, for whatever reason, are downright malicious. With these people, you could analyze them from Samhain to summer solstice and it isn't going to do you any good. To stop them in their tracks, and send that energy back, try this spell.

In various magickal systems throughout the world we find all manner of feather magick. In Egypt, the feather was used as a representation of Maat, the Mother of Justice, whose name meant "truth." Feathers are also a symbol of the element of air, which we will employ here. Maat was said not to judge herself, but to be supreme over the human conscience, making her a part of one's motivating force when we seek to do moral acts. Upon death, the heart would be placed on one side of a set of scales and the feather of Maat placed upon the other. In this way, one's deeds became one's entrance to the Elysian Fields if the scale balanced. If the scales did not balance, then you were considered unworthy and subsequently were consumed by Ammit.

Supplies: Black construction paper; 13 black feathers; glue; a small item that belongs to the mean person (a paper clip from his or her desk, or hair from a brush, or a signed credit card receipt, etc.).

Instructions: Cut a heart out of the black construction paper. Ring with black feathers, then glue in place. Glue the item belonging to the person on the back of the heart. Ask Maat to weigh the heart and protect you from negative actions and energies. Hide in a safe place until you are no longer targeted. Keep if you think they might bother you again. Destroy by fire if you think they've gone away or stopped for good.

A note of caution: Call on Maat only if you are positive that your own slate is clean, and that you have not caused your own difficulties.

Getting Rid of a Jealous Lover

In the beginning, you thought they were heaven-sent. Alas, alack, you'd like to give 'em back. Since fouled amour has no return policy attached to it, you might want to try this spell.

Supplies: A white candle; a black candle; your hair and hair from his or her brush; a pair of chopsticks; a thin, black, 13-inch-long ribbon; a cauldron or pot filled with sand.

Instructions: Place the two candles together on a table or altar. Make sure they are touching each other. The white candle stands for you, the black candle represents the other person. Light both candles, first visualizing yourself as you light the white candle, then visualizing the other person as you light the black candle. Take the hair from yourself and the other person and wrap around the chopsticks. Wind the black ribbon around the hair and chopsticks. Do not tie. Take a deep breath and visualize the other person walking (or running, if you prefer) away from you as you move the candles at least three inches apart. Then, when you feel you have the picture securely in your mind, burn the chopsticks in the cauldron. Move the candles apart again. Allow candles to burn completely. Dispose of everything in different places. Put your candle in your yard, the other person's candle off your property, and the chopstick pieces and sand in the garbage. This spell can take less than twenty-four hours (ask my daughter) or up to thirty days to work to completion. If your unwanted lover still hangs on, feel free to work the spell again. Sometimes a stubborn lover takes awhile to extricate from your life.

To enhance this spell:

- Perform this spell on the beach at dawn or sunset using small candles so that the ritual won't take as long.

- Entreat the assistance of a god or goddess of the sea.

Practical Tip

Most law enforcement personnel indicate that if someone tries to abduct you in a public place, you should
make a scene. That's right. Kick. Scream. Become a
maniac. It is more than likely your abductor will run
away if someone notices what is happening. Statistics
indicate that if your abductor gets you some place
alone, you will not survive.

Shrinking Evil

This is an old Pennsylvania Dutch Pow-Wow spell that takes approximately thirty days to work, though you will probably see the effects within the first week. Its prime directive is to dissipate evil from any home, office, farm, and so on. Pow-Wow is a magickal system that is approximately 300 years old, an amalgam of High German magick and folk application with tidbits of Native American practices.

Black pepper is made from the berries of the pepper plant and is considered one of the earliest known spices—indeed, the ransom of Rome was paid partly in pepper. Both black and white pepper come from the same source and both have been used for centuries in a variety of folk spells, especially in Pow-Wow magick. The turnip is considered a feminine plant, associated with the moon and earth magick, and is employed primarily for protection.

Supplies: 1 turnip; sharp knife; a tea candle; the name of the individual who is causing the problem, or the situation listed on a small piece of paper; sea salt (cleansing); black pepper (causing evil to flee); black marker.

Instructions: Cut the top off the turnip. Hollow out vegetable with a sharp knife, making a large enough indentation that the tea candle will fit down in the turnip. (This is going to take you awhile.) As you are working, concentrate on cutting the evil out of your life. Throw the turnip pieces at a crossroads at midnight (or as close to it as you can get). Put the piece of paper at the very bottom of the hole. Cover the paper with sea salt and visualize the manifestation of cleansing energy. Sprinkle black pepper on top (thinking of evil leaving your environment). Set the candle on the mixture. Use the black marker to ring the outside of the turnip with pentacles.

Hold your hands over the turnip. Visualize a white light glowing, and then growing around the turnip. Light the candle. Think of white light encompassing your environment, leaving no place for evil to hide. Allow the candle to burn completely. Remove the candle. Over the next thirty days the turnip will begin to shrink and collapse in onto itself. Do not remove until your environment feels free of negativity. When you feel comfortable, throw the turnip in the trash.

Practical Tip

What to expect when you call 911—if you are in a situation where you need to call for fire, police, or medical assistance, you need to be prepared to answer some specific questions. The operator will need a brief description of what has happened. They need to know where and when the incident occurred (or is occurring). Is anyone injured? Are there weapons involved? Are any suspects still in the area? What does the person/motor vehicle look like? Who are you (including your name, address, and phone number)? If you are reporting a crime or accident, you can remain anonymous, so don't call just because you don't want your name involved. Someone's life may depend on your action!

Candle Magick for Court Cases

Court case magick can get complicated. As a rule, the complications rise exponentially with each witness or player in the drama. Your attorney expects you to have detailed information and this will help you in your magick. For any court case magick, you will need to write on a piece of paper:

- The name of your attorney.

- The docket number of the case.

- The title of the case (e.g., Spot vs. Piewacket).

You should also try to get the business cards of your attorney and anyone else involved in the case. On another piece of paper, write down the names of the individual going to court against you, and the name of his or her attorney.

The energies of Jupiter are often used in legal matters, as Jupiter is seen as the Great Beneficent, carrying expansive energies. Jupiter's energy allows us to benefit from our inherent qualities and talents and, more importantly, helps us to recognize opportunities as they become available; therefore, this spell seeks out opportunities that will be beneficial to your case.

Other Supplies: 1 purple seven-day candle; 4 blue candles; a pin or nail; cinquefoil; powdered mustard; a brown candle for anyone testifying against you, or for a civil case; a gold candle for yourself if you are being sued; rose oil; a white candle for the judge (unless it is divorce court, then the candle for the judge should be red).

Instructions: Place the paper with your name, your attorney's name, the court docket number, and the name of the case under the purple seven-day candle. Inscribe the sign of Jupiter ($\u005C$) on the four blue candles with a pin or nail. Surround the purple candle with the blue candles. Say:

> The Goddess reigns supreme.
> She is clothed with the sun,
> the moon beneath her feet.
> She holds in her arms the strength of the universe.
> She cannot be dethroned.
> She is joy, truth, order, and hope.
> None can depose her.
> She is the beginning and the end of all things.

The God is my protector and my champion,
and lends his power to her.
The floods of discontent have lifted up against me,
threatening to engulf me.
The waves are the many voices of my enemies.
The Lord and Lady are mightier than the many
waves of mine enemies' sea.
My testimony and those who testify for me
will be sure, strong, and winning.
In the names of the Lord and Lady,
victory shall be mine!

Clap your hands to seal the spell. Sprinkle cinquefoil
and powdered mustard on the paper with the names of
those who are against you. Place the names of those
testifying against you under the brown candle.

Dress the judge's candle with rose oil. Place the name
of the judge under the white or red candle (depending
on what color you chose). Light all remaining candles,
and say:

Plead my cause, Goddess, with them
who strive against me. Fight against them
who wish to harm me, or who speak out against me.
Take hold of your shield and sword,
my Lady and Lord, and stand up for me.
Draw out the spear and stop the way
against those that persecute me.
Let them be confounded and shamed
that seek to hurt me. Let them be turned back
and brought to confusion that devise my pain.
Let them be as chaff before the wind;
and let their Karma chase them.
My Lady, Great Goddess of the angels,
send your messengers on the wild hunt,
seeking them out, bringing their actions to rest
in their own arms. Send them to the pit they,
themselves, have dug. Let their karmic destruction
come upon them at unawares and let their words
catch them and snare them in their own deceit.
Rescue me, my Lord and Lady, from this adversity.
Let not my enemies rejoice over me.

Let them be ashamed and brought to confusion
together that rejoice over my hurt;
let them be clothed with shame and dishonor,
and may it be magnified against them.
Rise up now, great Lord and Lady,
and deliver justice in my favor!
So mote it be.

Clap your hands to seal the spell. Allow all candles to
burn completely. **Note:** If you have a sword among your
magickal tools, then hold the sword above your head as
you repeat the last invocation.

To enhance this spell:

• Jupiter's energies are magnified by the full moon, therefore you greatly enhance the success of this spell if you
can perform it under this moon phase. When the energies of the moon and Jupiter are coupled, the combined
force is considered the luckiest moment for a magickal
working.

- If you are overwrought by circumstances, add the energies of the planet Venus to your working to put emotions to your advantage, especially if your situation is carried in the media.

- For an extra kick to a slow-moving case, add the energies of Mars, though be careful you don't inflame the issue.

Legal Assistance Powder

Supplies: Black pillar or votive candle; black talc; High John (protection); Low John (protection); cloves (protection); sage (protection and wisdom); rosemary (protection); pipe tobacco (purification); mortar and pestle; drill.

Instructions: On Tuesday (in the hour of Mars if you can, or when Mars is well aspected) mix the above ingredients to a fine powder with a mortar and pestle. Drill a hole in the bottom of the candle. Load with some of the powder. On your court date, sprinkle some of the powder in your shoes. While you are at court, make sure the black candle is at home, burning in the bathtub or kitchen sink.

Banish Media Lies

This very simple spell comes from West Virginia. In the old days (and there are those of us who can remember them) we did not use plastic bags (or disposals) to get rid of our garbage. Nope. Mom used to wrap the garbage in brown paper or old newsprint, then stuff the smelly parcel in the trash can. If someone has written you a nasty letter, or the media is trying to ruin your reputation, or some nut is just dancing plain havoc through your life, it's time to banish that negativity. This spell is best done on the dark of the moon.

Supplies: Your garbage (food is best because it rots); brown paper with the individual's name written on it; newsprint or the offending letter.

Instructions: Dump the garbage in the paper. Wrap it neatly, folding it repeatedly. Each time you make a fold, say:

> **Ghosts and goblins**
> **Bluebirds and robins**
> **Take back your crap**
> **You filthy rat**

Numb your tongue
Be deaf and dumb
May your voice fail
Now turn your tail!

Take the garbage to the dump.

To ☆Overcome Anger at Work

Your career is important. It represents many things (and some it shouldn't), including your self-worth, your perceptions of others, and your security. You can't perform well if you are angry. Try this spell to help you keep a clear head.

Supplies: Basil; chili powder; black pepper; angelica; a refillable mechanical pencil.

Instructions: Mix herbs together. Grind into a fine powder. Dump out the lead in the pencil. Replace with powder. Empower pencil to assist you in overcoming anger, and carry with you.

Practical Tip

It's okay to be mad. We do have emotions for a good reason (mainly to give us a vehicle to release stress). There have been occasions in my life when I've been so angry that I did not work magick because I knew that if I did, the person I was angry at would most likely end up in a morgue somewhere if I didn't walk away and calm down. It is natural to be furious—part of the human condition. As we get older, (hopefully) we mature and things that might have upset us in our teens and early adulthood no longer carry the same impact. A magickal group in Arizona trains their students to wait for seven days before working magick if a situation has made them ballistic, so there is time to think things through. This is a pretty good rule, and I've followed it myself many times. However, this doesn't mean you're supposed to be an unfeeling iceberg, nor does it mean that if you are in immediate trouble you can't work good, strong magick. Go ahead and work your magick (giving yourself time to think rationally), and remember that your job is to deflect negativity and ask for justice guided by the energy of Spirit.

To Catch a Thief

Although we often think that murder or rape catches the most statistics in the growing wave of criminal behavior, it is burglary and petty theft that take the top numbers in most American cities. Who better to call on than Hecate, Grecian goddess of knowledge, wealth, magick, moon, and the night? Our lady of the night was considered the queen of restless ghosts, believed to emerge when called, "entwined with fearsome serpents and leaves of oak, amidst a shimmering blaze of torchlight; while all around her hounds bayed shrilly, all the meadows trembled at her footfall, and the nymphs of marshland and river cried aloud."[3] Unfortunately, too many scholars in our time were quick to cast this powerful goddess in a malevolent light (much like the Celtic Morrigan), only to recently re-evaluate her standing among Roman/Greco

----

3. Robert Von Rudloff, *Hekate in Ancient Greek Religion* (Horned Owl Publishing: Victoria, Canada, 1999).

deities with a bit more professional savvy, attributing to her
the ability to bestow honors and good fortune among her
followers, as well as primary dominion over that portion of
existence the Witches call "Between the Worlds."

To catch a thief, use this great little spell.

Supplies: 1 black candle; a needle or nail; honey; spider
webs (real ones); a piece of paper with stolen items listed
on it.

Instructions: If you know the name of the thief
(absolutely, positively, no doubt in your mind), then
inscribe their name on the candle with a needle or nail.
If you are not 100 percent sure, please don't inscribe
anything. Coat the candle in honey, then roll in old
spider webs. (Heck, you needed to clean out that cubby-
hole in the basement, anyway.) Write what was stolen on
a piece of paper and set the paper under the candle. Say
the following:

**Hecate, Mother of Night, ruler of the moon
Sweep your dark skirts upon the one
Who has stolen from me.**

Turn your all-seeing eyes
Your burning orbs of wisdom
To bring focus on the thief.
Let no shred of darkness
No amount of cover hide them.
Come forth! Great Mother
of the Heavens and starry skies
Bring your justice!
Trap the thief in the web of their deceit!
And let them not rest
Until my things are returned
And justice is served.
So mote it be!

Allow the candle to burn completely. Burn the paper.

Note: You can also use this spell if someone has taken your job away from you, beat you out for a promotion unfairly, or moved into a position of authority that you had fairly earned.

Nailing a Criminal

This is an old folk spell that we've changed a bit. Originally, you were to nail the picture of the thief to a living tree. We've progressed since then to the understanding that trees are living entities and therefore don't deserve to be abused with hammer and nail. To catch a criminal (or someone who is doing nefarious, immoral deeds), try the following spell.

Supplies: Hammer; nails (coffin nails if you can get them); graveyard dirt (or the substitute version on page 159); a picture of the criminal (if you do not know who the criminal is, then list the crime(s) on a piece of paper).

Instructions: Under a full or new moon, take the hammer, nails, graveyard dirt, and picture outside. Nail the picture into the ground. Sprinkle with the graveyard dirt. Ask Spirit to help the proper authorities catch the criminal. (If a murder or other violent crime has occurred that was in the newspapers, you can use the newspaper article if you don't know who did it.) Sprinkle with the graveyard dirt. This spell takes approximately thirty days to manifest. If the criminal is not caught in thirty days, renew the graveyard dirt, again stating your petition. Continue until the issue is resolved.

To enhance this spell:

- Perform on a Saturday in the hour of Saturn.

- Perform on the dark of the moon.

- Design a shrine to Hecate for continued assistance when protection of home or family is needed.

Practical Tip

If you are the victim of a crime, try to remain calm. Do not show any signs of anger or confusion. If the attacker is after your purse or other valuable objects, don't resist. Make a conscious effort to get a description of your attacker. Practice matching words to things you see to help you remember. Call the police immediately. They will ask you for your name and where you are. Expect it. Contact your local victim assistance agency. You are not weak if you seek help.

Other Inventive Ideas to Catch Criminals

- Use a mousetrap. Spring the trap on the picture of the criminal, asking that the authorities discover the proper bait to use to catch them.

- Stuff the criminal's name or detail of the crime in a roach motel. Write the word "Jail" on the outside of the box with black marker.

- Load a black pillar candle with crushed nightshade. Carve the astrological sign of Saturn (♄), for constriction, on the black candle. Paint with a sticky substance, such as honey. Empower the candle to bring energies to catch the thief.

- Use fly or mouse paper. Write the crime or the criminal's name on the back of the paper. Create an effigy of the criminal with toothpicks and stick to the paper.

Practical Tip

Are there such things as moon-influenced crimes? Law enforcement officials think so. Just as the moon affects the tides of our oceans and manipulates our weather patterns, so does she fiddle with human emotions. Remember, the moon represents receptivity, and when full, she is in all her glory. It is no joke that through the history of humankind many spells were performed on the full moon. Why? The ancients knew the powerful forces that could manifest if combined and channeled in a useful way. Magickal people learn to capture the force of their own heightened emotional sensors under her influence, and to use that power to effect change. Workings under the full moon will carry more influence than at any other time of the month.

Experts have also noticed a slight increase in criminal behavior the three days prior the new moon as well.[4]

----

4. Lori Reid, *Moon Magic* (New York: Crown Publishers, Inc., 1998), p. 34.

Triple Action Protection Incense[5]

This is for those really nefarious cases. It has a powerful smell, so make sure the room is well fumigated. Best made on the full moon.

> **Supplies:** Mortar and pestle; 1 tablespoon copal resin; ½ tablespoon frankincense resin; 1 teaspoon myrrh resin; 3 pinches dragon's blood resin; 9 drops rue oil; ½ teaspoon crushed vervain; ¼ teaspoon crushed cinquefoil.

> **Directions:** In mortar and pestle, coarsely grind copal, frankincense, myrrh, and dragon's blood resins. Add rue oil and mix well. Add vervain and cinquefoil. Mix. Store in a jar or plastic bag. Add to charcoal to burn.

----

5. Made by Morgana of Morgana's Chamber.

Fearless Phantasm

There are times when a full ritual is required, rather than a spell. This particular ritual is used to bring stalkers, criminals, and abusers to justice. Goddesses of choice would be Kore (early Grecian), Hecate (Grecian), the Morrigan (Celtic), Sekhmet (Egyptian), or Kali. Kali is associated with various energies, including ceremonies, healing, time, death, courage, luck, education, knowledge, and war. She is seen as a primordial being and, as such, is incredibly powerful—a mother guardian for those who seek her assistance. She is a Hindu goddess and the symbol of eternal time. She gives life and she destroys it. Sometimes she is portrayed with the head of a jackal. Although much ado has been made about her aspects of destruction, she also soothes fears and provides a natural death to situations that have gotten out of hand. The Dark Mother of the Hindi, she is the triple goddess of creation, preservation, and destruction. Few Western scholars understood the profound philosophy of the Hindu belief in Kali, seeing her depicted as a man-hungry, man-hating demon, and thus have done her a great disservice over the years using

inaccurate interpretations. It is from this goddess, not the
Christians who eventually claimed it, that we have the
Creative Word. Kali reminds me of a stern Southern mother
(like mine) who might say, "I brought you into this world,
and I can take you out!" Kali is as her name means:
Becoming.

Supplies: Black illuminator candles; sage; 4 white candles
(votives will do); person's picture; 3 tapers (white, red,
and black—these are the colors of Kali, known as
Guanas: white for the Virgin, red for the Mother, and
black for the Crone); the person's name or the situation
written on a piece of parchment in
dragon's blood ink (To make
dragon's blood ink, mix 1 part
dragon's blood, 15 parts alcohol,
and 1 part gum arabic).

Setup: Place the two illuminator
candles on the altar. Sage the
room, or use triple action
protection incense. (If you are

a practicing magickal person, perform your full altar setup and rite of consecration.) Place the four votive candles at the quarters (north, east, south, and west) around the place where you will be performing the ritual. Put the picture of the person, their name, or description of the situation in the center or your altar or table. Inscribe the sign of Saturn (♄), the sign of Mars (♂), and the sign of Mercury (☿) on the three taper candles (red, white, and black). Set these candles on top of the picture, name, or issue. Light the illuminator candles if you have not done so already.

Circle casting: Cast your magickal circle by walking three times clockwise (deosil) around the room, saying:

> I conjure thee, O great circle of protection,
> So that you will be for me a boundary
> between the world of humans and
> the realms of the mighty spirits.
> A meeting place of perfect love, trust, peace, and joy.
> A cauldron of protective energies
> Containing the power I will raise herein.
> I call upon the guardians of the east,

the south, the west, and the north
to aid me in this consecration.
In the names of the Lord and Lady
thus do I conjure thee,
O great circle of protection!

When you are finished, stomp your foot, and say:

This circle is sealed.

Call the quarters: Go to each quarter, beginning in the north, and say:

Hail, Guardians of the North *(East, South, West)*,
I *(say your name)*
Do summon the element Earth *(Air, Fire, Water)*
Stir my ancestral dead
And call forth Spirit *(or you can insert a god
or goddess name that fits that quarter)*.
To witness this rite and protect this sacred space.
Hail and welcome!

As you move to each quarter, light the quarter candle.

Body of the ritual: Step forward and pick up the first of the unlit, inscribed candles. Hold this candle tightly in your hands. Visualize the perpetrator being caught for their crimes. Hold the candle until your fingers start to thump from the pressure. Take a deep breath and light the candle. Then, slowly, begin to walk the circle, asking for justice and protection from each quarter. Speak in your own words—the more impassioned, the better. When you have made one pass around the circle, move back to the altar, repeating the process with the other two inscribed candles, one at a time. With the last candle, move to the center. Hold up the candle as high as you can, and say:

Mighty Kali, terrible mother!
Goddess of creation, preservation, and destruction.
Dark mother, hear me! I call for justice!

Then explain to the goddess exactly what you need. Walk the circle again, saying:

I conjure a phantasm
Outside of this circle be.
I conjure a phantasm

To bring justice to thee.
I conjure a phantasm
To haunt your every move
To keep you from harming another poor fool.
I conjure a phantasm
To ruin your all your plans.
I conjure a phantasm
To search throughout the land.
I conjure a phantasm
With teeth and wings and fire.
I conjure a phantasm
To do as I desire!
I conjure this phantasm
To bring your evil down
I conjure this phantasm
To move without a sound.
I conjure a phantasm
To sniff out your hate, and greed, and sin.
I conjure a phantasm
To pull the justice in!

Keep walking the circle, saying:

> **Be off with you now**
> **My phantasm of justice**
> **Find** *(person's name)*
> **And bring their Karma to bear!**
> **Return to the ether when your job is done.**

Lift your arms in the air and visualize the phantasm lifting outside of the circle and zooming to do his duty. Expect things to crash around outside (it happens), but you are safe inside of the circle. Thank Kali for her assistance. Close up the circle by dismissing the quarters (counterclockwise or widdershins). Take up the circle in your hand, once around, counterclockwise. Stamp your foot, and say:

> **This circle is open,**
> **but never broken!**

Allow all candles to burn completely.

To enhance this spell:

• Perform near the ocean, seen as a representation of the great abyss from which Kali birthed the human race (the primordial deep).

• Add seashells, sand, and other representations of the sea to your altar.

When It Gets Pretty Deep: The Rite of Thesmophoria

Thesmophoria is actually the name for an ancient ceremony of honor focusing on the law and justice in the name of the Grecian goddess Demeter. You will need an athame (magickal knife or dagger) for this ritual.

Supplies: Mortar and pestle; allspice (healing); orris (protection); patchouli (lust); cinnamon (power); sandalwood (wishes); clove (exorcism); 1 black pillar candle; situation or person's name written on a piece of paper, or a photograph; a bowl of honey; a bowl of milk; 2 taper candles; 4 brown votive candles dressed in protection oil; a picture of a loving goddess (we are using Demeter for this one, but you could choose a different goddess if you like); athame.

Setup: Mix allspice, orris, patchouli, cinnamon, sandalwood, and clove with mortar and pestle into a fine powder. Load some of the powder into the bottom of the black pillar candle. Save the remainder and set aside. Put the paper or picture in the center of your altar. Place the black pillar candle on top. Put the milk to the right and the honey to the left of the black pillar candle. Complete setting up the altar using the brown taper candles for illuminator candles. (Magickal people can use their familiar altar devotion and altar setup.) Cleanse and consecrate the altar. Put the quarter candles at the compass points of your circle—north, east, south, and west.

Circle casting: Walk the circle once clockwise (deosil), and say:

> **Around and about me**
> **Above and below me**
> **I conjure a circle of protection and power.**

North and east, south and west
I add these energies to my enchantment.
O great circle of art, I conjure thee now!
And legions await my word!
This circle is sealed.

Call the quarters: Go to each quarter, beginning in the north, and say:

Hail, Guardians of the north *(east, south, west)*,
I *(say your name)*
Do summon the element Earth *(Air, Fire, Water)*
Stir my ancestral dead
And call forth Spirit *(or you can insert a god or goddess name that fits that quarter).*
To witness this rite and protect this sacred space.
Hail and welcome!

As you move to each quarter, light the quarter's candle.

Calling Spirit: Stand at the center of your circle. You will now call on Demeter by holding your arms up straight over your head and repeating the following (or words of your choice):

Holy Mother
She of many faces and many names
Bright Mother
Come now to my rite of Thesmophoria
Great Mother
She of fair and equal justice
I ask for your intercession
I give to you the sacrifice of milk and honey
I call you forth into this circle
to assist me in my time of need!

The body of the ritual: State the purpose of your ritual, then dip the athame first in the milk, then in the honey. Hold your athame over the candle, and say:

Queen of the Moon
Queen of the Stars
Queen of the Horns
Queen of the Fires
Queen of Earth
Bring to me the justice I seek

> For it is you, bright Lady
> Who gives birth to the Hidden Children.[6]

Light the pillar candle. Hold the athame over your head,
then slowly bring it down to the flame, and say:

> Gracious Goddess
> Holy and Divine
> Answer to the call of nine!
> One—I stand before thy throne,
> Two—I invoke thee alone!
> Three—I hold aloft my blade,
> Four—Descend! The spell is made!
> Five—Lend thy gift to give it life.
> Six—Thy unwielding strength into my knife.
> Seven—On earth, in sky, and sea,
> O gracious Goddess, be with me!
> Eight—Come now as the call is made,
> Nine—Give thy power unto my blade![7]

----

6. Jessie Wicker Bell, *Grimoire of Lady Sheba* (St. Paul, Minn.:
   Llewellyn, 1972).
7. Ibid.

Poise the blade over the candle flame and think of the justice that you seek. Allow the power to flow through you until you reach an altered state, then think once more of the justice you seek, take a deep breath, and plunge the blade into the pillar candle (be careful not to burn yourself). Then say:

So be it ardane!

Remove the blade. Thank deity. Close quarters by thanking them and wishing them farewell. Take up the circle in your hand in a counterclockwise direction. Put this energy into the candle by holding your hand over the flame (not too close) and visualizing the power of the circle entering the candle. Say:

This circle is open, but never broken!

Clap your hands or stomp your foot. Clean your blade. Allow the candle to burn completely. Offer the milk and honey to the animals on your property. When the candle has finished burning, break the pieces and scatter at a crossroads.

Practical Tip

Date rape is a serious crime that is confusing and often goes without the victim reporting the crime. Rape, regardless who commits the act against a woman or man, is a felony sexual assault that leaves the victim injured and traumatized. Victims of rape, especially when that rape is committed by someone they know, often feel that it is their fault, assuming false responsibility for the attack. Therefore, the crime often goes unreported. To avoid date rape: if you don't know your date well, drive your own car, or better yet, double date. Communicate your limits firmly and clearly. Don't rely on ESP to get your message across. Stay sober. Listen to your inner self. Don't be afraid to make a scene if you feel threatened. Attend large parties with friends you can trust. If you are a victim of rape—don't wait. Contact the authorities immediately. If you wait, valuable evidence will be lost, and the chance of successfully prosecuting your case may be endangered.

Practical Tip

In dealing with domestic violence, doing nothing solves nothing. It is a crime to threaten another person. Don't stay in your home, get to a safe place. Call a twenty-four-hour battered women's hotline. Call the police. If you are in this situation, do not think that you can control it. Follow through on your call. Write down the detective's name that is handling your case. Don't ever believe "I'll never hit you again." Think about your future! If the batterer refuses to seek help, it is unlikely that the beatings will stop. Even if you have never worked before, you can become self-supporting. Don't stay in a bad situation because you think you have nowhere else to go. You do. Refusing to look at the situation is called denial. Seek counseling after you have gotten out. A large percentage of women go back because they have not had appropriate counseling. A victim of domestic violence has often been brainwashed by the offending party over a period of time, often years. The victim needs to be reprogrammed for her health and continued survival. I ought to know. Twenty-two years ago, I was a battered wife. You can make it. I did.

When Things Get Deeper Still: The Rite of the Furies

Although this rite works well for all sorts of nasty circumstances, it was originally designed for parents whose children have in some way been harmed by a person or a group of people, or for a woman who is the victim of domestic abuse. The Furies are, perhaps, the oldest images of Greek matriarchal law. This triple goddess combination punishes transgressors who have acted against a maternal line, and were originally called the Erinyes (the Avengers). These are the Daughters of Earth and Shadow, thought to be the most ancient of spirits, perhaps stemming from the belief in ancestral spirits or angry ghosts of the murdered. They will not desist until the expiation of the crime. To see them is to witness strong, determined women carrying weapons of slaughter. As with the last ritual, milk and honey are considered acceptable offerings to these deities.

Supplies: Anointing oil; a bell; an empty journal book; a red pen; a black candle.

Instructions: Anoint your forehead, breastbone, left
shoulder, right shoulder, and forehead (again). Cast a
magick circle. Hold your palms together at chest level.
Close your eyes and breathe deeply for at least one
minute. Concentrate on the light of the universe focusing on the criminal(s). It's okay if you can't see their
faces, just concentrate on universal truth infusing the
circle and the situation.

Put your hands down at your sides and move your feet
apart. Slowly, raise your arms, accepting the holy light
into your body. Say:

> **Daughters of Earth and Shadow.**
> **Avengers of the universe, hear my plea!**

Ring the bell. Place your hands on the open journal
book and, with the red pen, poise over the pages. Say:

> **As I write the name of the criminal,**
> **I ask for justice!**

Write the name. Ring the bell three times. Hold your
hands over the black candle, and say:

As I light this candle,
I bring forth justice!

Light the candle. Ring the bell three times. Put the bell
and the candle on top of the book. Stand back, begin to
clap your hands, and say:

> **Bell, book, and candle;**
> **no more victims, no more scoundrel.**
> **Bell, book, and candle;**
> **Furies right and furies left;**
> **catch them now, justice met;**
> **Bell, book, and candle.**

Keep chanting, envisioning the Furies coming down
from the heavens and snatching up the criminal(s). If
you have a drum or rattle, you might want to use the
instrument to help you raise power.

When you are finished, ring the bell three times.
Release the circle. Allow the candle to burn to
completion. When the criminal has been caught and
brought to justice, burn the book. Do not use the book
for any other purpose.

Tips for Reporting Suspicious Activities

So what's this stuff doing in a magickal book? Just because you want to do spells does not mean that you should practice selective awareness. If you are the witness to a crime or you observe suspicious activity, here are things you should try to remember.

For a vehicle:

- License plate number and state.

- Color of vehicle.

- Body style (2-door, 4-door, SUV, pickup, convertible).

- Location and direction of travel.

- Description of occupants.

For a person:

- Race.

- Gender.

- Clothing: hat, jacket, shirt, pants, shoes, dress, blouse, skirt.

- Unusual habit or odd characteristic.

- Facial features: hair color, hair length, facial hair, glasses, scars, missing teeth, height, weight, location and direction the person was heading.

Be alert. Be aware. Be confident!

Working Things Out

Whenever unfortunate things happen to us, we carry our anger and frustration inside of us. Although we may get involved and do things to change the system that allowed something to occur, we still need to funnel that anger. If we do not deal with our negative emotions, one of the following is most likely to happen:

- You will get sick—cold, flu, or something worse. I've noticed a number of back injuries over the years that actually coincide with traumatic events in a person's life where they thought that the fate of the world was balanced upon their shoulders, and that they would eventually lose.

- Your personality will reflect negativity, bitterness, and so on. You meet these people all the time, don't you? When I hear of a particularly nasty person, I always wonder what event (or events) brought them to this juncture in life.

- The negativity of your anger affects your environment, pulling you closer to poverty or whatever your deepest fear may be.

- You completely bury the anger in your subconscious where it may manifest years later in an emotionally crippling way.

Over the years I have collected several ideas on how to deal with anger.

- Weave the negativity into cords that you can burn or vines that you can throw into a living body of water.

- Sit down. Put your shoulders back, breathe deeply several times, and imagine that the negative energy is leaving your body, and positive energy is entering. Shoulders still back, extend your right arm so that it is parallel to the floor and stretch those muscles. Turn the palm up and down while stretching. Try not to overstretch. Slowly bring that arm over to rest in your lap, palm of the hand cupped as if you are holding the waters of life. Now do the same thing with your left arm. Take a deep breath and let yourself sink into relaxation. You can spend as much time in this position as you like. Use to begin or end any meditation or visualization sequence. This is also a nice exercise before or after a daily altar devotion.

- Banish your anger by writing a letter that details your feelings. Call the Roman goddess Vesta, asking for cleansing and purification, then burn the letter in a ritual fire.

Tying Things Up

There will be instances where, although the worst is over, there are loose ends to be handled. Many times we try to avoid those little wigglers, but they'll come back to haunt us so we might as well do something about it. If these loose ends involve another person that you are still speaking to, then you may wish, as a unit, to do this spell; for instance, two friends who have had a blowup, have resolved the worst, and now must work out the rest of the issues if they are to keep their relationship.

Supplies: Several yards of black ribbon; a small paper plate; a hole punch; tissues (if you are doing this with a partner—trust me, you'll need them); a plastic resealable bag large enough to hold the plate.

Instructions: Cast a circle and call the quarters. Ask for the attendance of Spirit. Carefully count out pieces of ribbon, 13 inches long, that match the number of issues unresolved, plus one ribbon for the "unknown"—something you forgot or just don't recognize right now. Punch the matching number of holes in a circular pattern around the small plate. Thread each ribbon through a hole, visualizing the issues as resolved. Tie a knot at both ends of the ribbon, and say:

The circulation of anger, hatred, and hurt is cut off.
I shall not be carried off by the flow of negativity.
So be it ardane!

If you are doing this with a partner for whom you need resolution, expect to bawl. The catharsis experienced by tears is good for the soul, so don't bother to hold back.

When finished, offer the beribboned plate to the universe, asking for closure. Place in a plastic resealable bag. You can add healing herbs to the contents of the bag if you like. Bury off your property.

Practical Tip

If you are a victim of a violent crime, you will most likely experience lasting emotional effects. Do not suppress your feelings of anger and frustration. There are a number of agencies in your area that will be willing to help you work through this unfortunate event. There is nothing to be ashamed of. If you are a friend or relative of a victim, please lend your emotional support and be available to listen. It might be wise if you also contact help agencies (check to see if your insurance has a phone helpline service available) so that you are armed with the appropriate responses that your friend or loved one may need. In most states in America, if you are a victim of domestic violence, you have the right to go to court and file a petition requesting a Protection from Abuse order. For more information, call your regional Domestic Violence Program.

Epilogue

It is my sincere hope that the spells and practical ideas in this book enhance your life in a positive, productive way. I'd like to remind you that these spells should not be substituted for intelligent action in any situation, and should not take the place of proper medical or legal counsel.

And remember, don't call up what you can't put down, real or otherwise.

Love,

Silver RavenWolf

Appendices

Appendix 1: Herbal Table

Herbs of Protection

Angelica	Ivy
Asafetida	Mandrake
Basil	Marigold
Bay Laurel	Mistletoe
Boneset	Nettle
Cinnamon	Rosemary
Cloves	Rue
Comfrey	Sage
Coxcomb	St. John's Wort
Fennel	Slippery Elm
Garlic	Solomon's Seal
Holly	Sunflower
Horehound	Vervain
Hound's Tongue	Yarrow

Herbs to Break Hexes

Angelica	Nightshade
Hemlock	Rue
Henbane	Solomon's Seal
Horehound	Yew
Nettle	Yarrow

Herbs of House and Business Blessing

Angelica	Lavender
Basil	Mandrake
Bay Laurel	Orris
Camphor	Orange Peel
Cinquefoil	Pine
Cowslip	Plantain
Elderflower	Rosemary
Figwort	Rowan
Garlic	Rue

Herbs of Exorcism

Angelica	Mint
Basil	Mistletoe
Clove	Myrrh
Cumin	Pepper
Dragon's Blood	Pine
Frankincense	Rosemary
Fumitory	Rue
Garlic	Sagebrush
Heliotrope	Sandalwood
Horehound	Snapdragon
Juniper	Thistle
Lilac	Yarrow
Mallow	

Appendix 2: Color Magick Correspondences

Use the lists below when in doubt, but don't view this information as the last word on color magick.

Color Magick Correspondence List

Color	Purpose
Black	Returning to sender; divination; negative work; protection
Blue-Black	For wounded pride; broken bones; angelic protection
Dark Purple	Used for calling up the power of the ancient ones; sigils/runes; government
Lavender	To invoke righteous spirit within yourself and favors for people
Dark Green	Invoking the goddess of regeneration; agriculture; financial
Mint Green	Financial gains (used with gold and silver)
Green	Healing or health; north cardinal point
Avocado Green	Beginnings
Light Green	Improve the weather
Indigo Blue	To reveal deep secrets; protection on the astral levels; defenses
Dark Blue	To create confusion (must be used with white or you will confuse yourself)
Blue	Protection
Royal Blue	Power and protection
Pale/Light Blue	Protection of home; buildings; young; young males

Color	Purpose
Ruby Red	Love or anger of a passionate nature
Red	Love; romantic atmosphere; energy; south cardinal point
Light Red	Deep affection of a nonsexual nature
Deep Pink	Harmony and friendship in the home
Pink	Harmony and friendship with people; binding magick
Pale Pink	Friendship; young females
Yellow	Healing; can also represent east cardinal point
Deep Gold	Prosperity; sun magick
Gold	Attraction
Pale Gold	Prosperity in health
Burnt Orange	Opportunity
Orange	Material gain; to seal a spell; attraction
Dark Brown	Invoking earth for benefits
Brown	Peace in the home; herb magick; friendship
Pale Brown	Material benefits in the home
Silver	Quick money; gambling; invocation of the moon; moon magick
Off-White	Peace of mind
Lily White	Mother Candle (burned for thirty minutes at each moon phase)
White	Righteousness; purity, used for east cardinal point; devotional magick
Gray	Glamouries

Use white to substitute for any color.

Colors for Days of the Week

Day	Color
Monday	White
Tuesday	Red
Wednesday	Purple
Thursday	Green
Friday	Blue
Saturday	Black
Sunday	Yellow

Appendix 3: Astrological Symbols

Use for carving on candles.

Zodiac Name	Glyph	Meaning
Aries	♈	To begin a project
Taurus	♉	To gain and keep luxury
Gemini	♊	To create communicative change
Cancer	♋	To work on positive emotions
Leo	♌	To guard what you have
Virgo	♍	To remember the details
Libra	♎	To bring fairness
Scorpio	♏	To intensify anything
Sagittarius	♐	To bring humor and friends
Capricorn	♑	To plan business finances
Aquarius	♒	To bring change and freedom
Pisces	♓	To connect to the spiritual world

PLANETS AND THEIR MEANINGS

Sun = Success

Moon = Family

Venus = Love and fast cash

Mars = To activate anything

Mercury = Communication

Jupiter = Expansion

Saturn = Banish or restrict

Appendix 4: Planetary Hours[1]

The selection of an auspicious time for beginning a magickal working is an important matter. When a thing is begun, its existence takes on the nature of the conditions under which it was begun.

Each hour of the day is ruled by a planet, and takes on the attributes of that planet. You will notice that planetary hours do not take into account Uranus, Neptune, and Pluto, as they are considered here as higher octaves of Mercury, Venus, and Mars, respectively. For example, if something is ruled by Uranus, you can use the hour of Mercury.

The only other factor you need to know to use the planetary hours is the time of your local sunrise and sunset for any given day, available from your local newspaper. **Note:** Your sunrise and sunset time may vary from the example if you live in a different location. Your latitude/longitude are already figured into your local paper's sunrise and sunset times.

---

1. Planetary hour information is condensed from *Llewellyn's 2000 Daily Planetary Guide*, pp. 184–185.

Step One. Find the sunrise and sunset times for your location for your chosen day from your local paper. We will use January 2, 1999, 10 degrees latitude, as an example. Sunrise for January 2, 1999, at 10 degrees latitude is at 6 hours and 16 minutes (or 6:16 A.M.) and sunset is at 17 hours and 49 minutes (or 5:49 P.M.).

Step Two. Subtract sunrise time (6 hours 16 minutes) from sunset time (17 hours 49 minutes) to get the number of astrological daylight hours. It is easier to do this if you convert the hours into minutes. For example, 6 hours and 16 minutes equals 376 minutes. 17 hours and 49 minutes equals 1,069 minutes. Now subtract: 1,069 minutes minus 376 minutes equals 693 minutes.

Step Three. Next you should determine how many minutes are in a daylight planetary hour for that particular day. To do this, divide 693 minutes (the number of daylight minutes) by 12. The answer is 58, rounded off. Therefore, a daylight planetary hour for January 2, 1999, at 10 degrees latitude has 58 minutes.

Step Four. Now you know that each daylight planetary hour is roughly 58 minutes. You also know, from step one, that sunrise is at 6:16 A.M. To determine the starting times of each planetary hour, simply add 58 minutes to the sunrise time for the first planetary hour, 58 minutes to that number for the second planetary hour, etc. Therefore, the first hour in our example is 6:16 A.M.–7:14 A.M. The second hour is 7:14 A.M.–8:12 A.M.; and so on. Note that because you rounded up the number of minutes in a sunrise hour, that the last hour doesn't end exactly at sunset. This is a good reason to give yourself a little "fudge space" when using planetary hours. (You could also skip the rounding-up step.)

Step Five. Now, to determine which sign rules which daylight planetary hour, consult your calendar to determine which day of the week January 2 falls on. You'll find it's a Saturday in 1999. Next, turn to page 239 to find the sunrise planetary hour chart. If you follow down the column for Saturday, you will see that the first hour is ruled by Saturn, the second by Jupiter, the third by Mars, and so on.

Step Six. Now you've determined the daytime (sunrise) planetary hours. You can use the same formula to determine the night-time (sunset) planetary hours, using sunset as your beginning time and sunrise the next day as your end time. When you get to step 5, remember to consult the sunset table on page 240 rather than the sunrise one.

Planetary Hours
Sunrise

Hour	Sunday	Monday	Tuesday	Wednesday	Thursday	Friday	Saturday
1	Sun	Moon	Mars	Mercury	Jupiter	Venus	Saturn
2	Venus	Saturn	Sun	Moon	Mars	Mercury	Jupiter
3	Mercury	Jupiter	Venus	Saturn	Sun	Moon	Mars
4	Moon	Mars	Mercury	Jupiter	Venus	Saturn	Sun
5	Saturn	Sun	Moon	Mars	Mercury	Jupiter	Venus
6	Jupiter	Venus	Saturn	Sun	Moon	Mars	Mercury
7	Mars	Mercury	Jupiter	Venus	Saturn	Sun	Moon
8	Sun	Moon	Mars	Mercury	Jupiter	Venus	Saturn
9	Venus	Saturn	Sun	Moon	Mars	Mercury	Jupiter
10	Mercury	Jupiter	Venus	Saturn	Sun	Moon	Mars
11	Moon	Mars	Mercury	Jupiter	Venus	Saturn	Sun
12	Saturn	Sun	Moon	Mars	Mercury	Jupiter	Venus

Planetary Hours
Sunset

Hour	Sunday	Monday	Tuesday	Wednesday	Thursday	Friday	Saturday
1	Jupiter	Venus	Saturn	Sun	Moon	Mars	Mercury
2	Mars	Mercury	Jupiter	Venus	Saturn	Sun	Moon
3	Sun	Moon	Mars	Mercury	Jupiter	Venus	Saturn
4	Venus	Saturn	Sun	Moon	Mars	Mercury	Jupiter
5	Mercury	Jupiter	Venus	Saturn	Sun	Moon	Mars
6	Moon	Mars	Mercury	Jupiter	Venus	Saturn	Sun
7	Saturn	Sun	Moon	Mars	Mercury	Jupiter	Venus
8	Jupiter	Venus	Saturn	Sun	Moon	Mars	Mercury
9	Mars	Mercury	Jupiter	Venus	Saturn	Sun	Moon
10	Sun	Moon	Mars	Mercury	Jupiter	Venus	Saturn
11	Venus	Saturn	Sun	Moon	Mars	Mercury	Jupiter
12	Mercury	Jupiter	Venus	Saturn	Sun	Moon	Mars

Appendix 5: Moon Phases

New Moon

- Moon is 0–45 degrees directly ahead of the sun
- Moon rises at dawn, sets at sunset; for full use of these energies, stick between this time period
- Moon is from exact new moon to 3½ days after
- Purpose: Beginnings
- Workings for: Beauty, health, self-improvement, farms and gardens, job hunting, love and romance, networking, creative ventures
- Pagan Holiday: Winter Solstice (December 22)[2]
- Goddess Name: Rosemerta's Moon
- Goddess Energy: Goddesses of Growth
- Offering: Milk and honey
- Theme: Abundance
- Rune: Feoh for abundance; Cen for openings; Gyfu for love
- Tarot Trump: The Fool

----

2. Due to astrological timing, solstices and equinoxes will not always be on the same date. Other Pagan holidays will differ depending on the tradition practiced.

Crescent

- Moon is 45–90 degrees ahead of the sun
- Moon rises at midmorning, sets after sunset; for full use of these energies, stick between this time period
- Moon is from 3½ to 7 days after the new moon
- Purpose: The movement of the thing
- Workings: Animals, business, change, emotions, matriarchal strength
- Pagan Holiday: Imbolc (February 1)
- Goddess Name: Brigid's Moon
- Goddess Energy: Water Goddesses
- Offering: Candles
- Theme: Manifestation
- Rune: Birca for beginnings; Ing for focus
- Tarot Trump: The Magician

First Quarter

- Moon is 90–135 degrees ahead of the sun
- Moon rises at noon, sets at midnight; for full use of these energies, stick between this time period
- Moon is from 7 to 10½ days after the new moon
- Purpose: The shape of the thing
- Workings: Courage, elemental magick, friends, luck, and motivation

- Pagan Holiday: Spring Equinox (March 21)
- Goddess Name: Persephone's Moon
- Goddess Energy: Air Goddesses
- Offering: Feathers
- Theme: Luck
- Rune: Algiz for luck; Jera for improvement; Ur for strength
- Tarot Card: Strength or The Star

Gibbous

- Moon is 135–180 degrees ahead of the sun
- Moon rises in midafternoon, sets around 3 A.M.; for full use of these energies, stick between this time period
- Moon is between 10½ to 14 days after the new moon
- Purpose: Details
- Workings: Courage, patience, peace, harmony
- Pagan Holiday: Beltaine (May 1)
- Goddess Name: Nuit's Moon
- Goddess Energy: Star Goddesses
- Offering: Ribbons
- Theme: Perfection
- Rune: Asa for eloquence; Wyn for success; Dag for enlightenment
- Tarot Trump: The World

Full Moon

- Moon is 180–225 degrees ahead of the sun
- Moon rises at sunset, sets at dawn; for full use of these energies, stick between this time period
- Moon is from 14 to 17½ days after the new moon
- Purpose: Completion of a project
- Workings: Artistic endeavors, beauty, health, fitness, change, decisions, children, competition, dreams, families, health, knowledge, legal undertakings, love, romance, money, motivation, protection, psychic power, self-improvement
- Pagan Holiday: Summer Solstice (June 21)
- Goddess Name: Sekhmet's Moon
- Goddess Energy: Fire Goddesses
- Offering: Flowers
- Theme: Power
- Rune: Sol
- Tarot Card: The Sun

Disseminating

- Moon is 225–270 degrees ahead of the sun
- Moon rises at midevening, sets at midmorning; for full use of these energies, stick between this time frame
- Moon is 3½ to 7 days after the moon
- Purpose: Initial destruction
- Working: Addiction, decisions, divorce, emotions, stress, protection

- Pagan Holiday: Lammas (August 1)
- Goddess Name: Hecate's Moon
- Goddess Energy: Earth Goddesses
- Offering: Grain or rice
- Theme: Reassessment
- Rune: Thorn for destruction; Algiz for protection; Thorn for defense
- Tarot Trump: The Tower for destruction; Hope for protection

Last Quarter

- Moon is 270–315 degrees ahead of the sun
- Moon rises at midnight and sets at noon; for full use of these energies, stick between this time frame.
- Moon is 7 to 10½ days after the full moon
- Purpose: Absolute destruction
- Working: Addictions, divorce, endings, health and healing (banishing), stress, protection, ancestors
- Pagan Holiday: Fall Equinox (September 21)
- Goddess Name: The Morrigan's Moon
- Goddess Energy: Harvest Goddesses
- Offering: Incense
- Theme: Banishing
- Rune: Hagal; Ken for banishing; Nyd for turning; Isa for binding
- Tarot Trump: Judgement

Balsamic (Dark Moon)

- Moon is 315–360 degrees ahead of the sun
- Moon rises at 3 A.M., sets midafternoon; for full use of these energies, stick between this time frame
- Moon is 10½ to 14 days after the full moon
- Purpose: Rest
- Working: Addictions, change, divorce, enemies, justice, obstacles, quarrels, removal, separation, stopping stalkers and theft
- Pagan Holiday: Samhain (October 31)
- Goddess Name: Kali's Moon
- Goddess Energy: Dark Goddesses
- Offering: Honesty
- Theme: Justice
- Rune: Tyr for justice; Ken for banishing
- Tarot Trump: Justice

Bibliography

Biederman, Hans. *Dictionary of Symbols.* Meridian, 1994 translation.

Cunningham, Scott. *Cunningham's Encyclopedia of Magical Herbs.* St. Paul, Minn.: Llewellyn, 1992.

Dixon-Kennedy, Mike. *Celtic Myth & Legend, An A-Z of People and Places.* London, England: Blandford Publishing, 1996.

Hopman, Ellen Evert. *A Druid's Herbal for the Sacred Earth Year.* Rochester, VT: Destiny Books, 1995.

Imel, Martha Ann & Dorothy Myers. *Goddesses in World Mythology.* New York: Oxford University Press, 1993.

Jones, Allison. *Larousse Dictionary of World Folklore.* Edinborough, England: Larousse, 1995.

Leach, Maria, ed. *Funk & Wagnall's Standard Dictionary of Folklore, Mythology, and Legend.* San Francisco: Harper SanFrancisco, 1972.

Leek, Sybil. *Sybil Leek's Book of Curses.* Englewood Cliffs, N.J.: Prentice-Hall, Inc., 1975.

———. *How To Be Your Own Astrologer.* New York: Cowles Book Company, Inc., 1970.

Liungman, Carl G. *Dictionary of Symbols.* New York: W. W. Norton & Co., 1991.

Martin, Richard. *Bulfinch's Mythology.* New York: HarperCollins, 1991.

Mercatante, Anthony S. *Facts on File Encyclopedia of World Mythology and Legend.* New York: Oxford, 1988.

Mickaharic, Draja. *Spiritual Cleansing.* York Beach, ME: Samuel Weiser, 1982.

Randolph, Vance. *Ozark Magic and Folklore.* New York: Dover Publications, 1947.

RavenWolf, Silver. *To Light a Sacred Flame.* St. Paul, Minn.: Llewellyn Publications, 1999.

Reid, Lori. *Moon Magic.* New York: Crown Publishers, Inc., 1998.

Rose, Carol. *Spirits, Fairies, Leprechauns, and Goblins—An Encyclopedia.* New York: W. W. Norton & Co., 1996.

Sjoestedt, Marie-Louise. *Gods and Heroes of the Celts.* Berkeley, Calif.: Turtle Island Foundation, 1982.

Slater, Herman. *Magickal Formulary Spellbook, Book II.* New York: Magickal Childe, n.d.

Sophia. *The Little Book of Hexes for Women.* Kansas City: Andrews McMeel Publishing, 1997.

Walker, Barbara. *The Woman's Dictionary of Symbols and Sacred Objects.* San Francisco: Harper Collins, 1988.

———. *The Woman's Encyclopedia of Myths and Secrets.* San Francisco: Harper SanFrancisco, 1983.

Wilde, Lady. *Irish Cures, Mystic Charms & Superstitions.* New York: Sterling Publishing, 1991.

Index